Moctezuma II, the Aztec emperor, certainly thought so. This tragic mistake led not only to the deadly clash of two diametrically opposed cultures, but also to the turning of a decisive page in world history. Bernal Díaz del Castillo, Cortés' faithful companion and chronicler, reported this crucial episode.

"We arrived at the Río de Grijalva, which in the Indian language is called the Tabasco River. We reached it with all our fleet on 12 March 1519.... More than 12,000 warriors had gathered.... With great bravery they surrounded us in their canoes and poured a shower of arrows on us....

"Juan de Escalante, the *alguacil mayor* [chief constable],…was
immediately sent [by Cortés]…to bring ashore all the anchors, cables,
sails, and other things that might be useful, and then destroy the ships.

"Moctezuma, the great and powerful prince of Mexico, in dread that we might come to his city, sent five chieftains of the highest rank to our camp…to bid us welcome…. He sent a present…worth about a thousand golden piasters….

"When we entered the town [of Tlaxcala], there was no room in the streets or on the roofs, so many men and women having come out with happy faces to see us.... We marched into Tlaxcala on 23 September 1519.

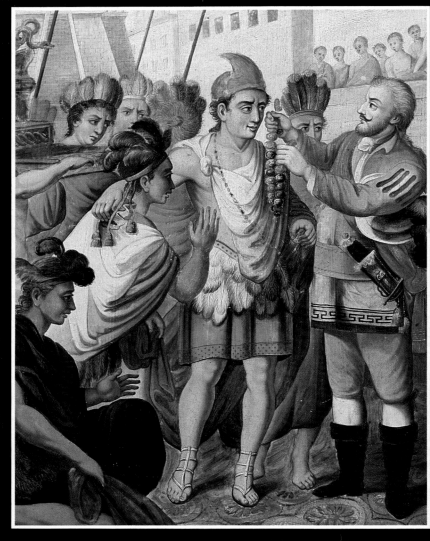

"When [Cortés] came near to Moctezuma each bowed deeply to the other.... Cortés brought out a necklace of elaborately worked and colored glass beads called *margaritas*.... This he hung around the great Moctezuma's neck.

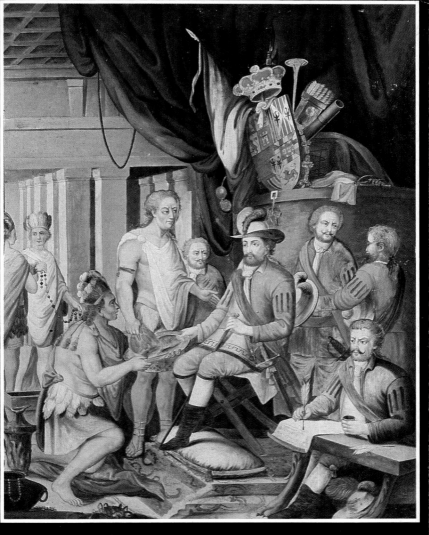

"When we had finished our meal, Moctezuma…came to our quarters in the grandest state with a great number of princes, all of them his kinsmen…. The great Moctezuma had some fine gold jewels of various shapes in readiness, which he gave to Cortés after this conversation.

"Captain Juan de Escalante, an ardent and vigorous man…prepared the most active and able-bodied soldiers among those who were left to him.… He went off to face the Mexican garrisons. The opposing forces found themselves face to face at daybreak.

"On entering the palace, Cortés made his usual salutations, and said to Moctezuma: 'If you cry out, or raise any commotion, you will immediately be killed by these captains of mine, whom I have brought for this sole purpose.'"

CONTENTS

THE AZTECS
RISE AND FALL OF AN EMPIRE

Serge Gruzinski

DISCOVERIES

HARRY N. ABRAMS, INC., PUBLISHERS

In the early chronicles of the history of the Mexican people, one image constantly arises—the great city of Tula. Abandoned in the 12th century, Tula, the erstwhile capital of the Toltec civilization, left its mark on the entire history of ancient Mexico.

CHAPTER I

TULA, THE MYTHICAL BEGINNING

A 16th-century depiction of the earliest stage in the history of the Mexica (the Aztecs), the start of their migration, when they lived in caves and hunted for food (left).

M an's head in stone (right) with eyes of pink mother-of-pearl encrusted with circles of pyrite and teeth of white mother-of-pearl.

Over the last two thousand years, several sophisticated civilizations have developed, flourished, and collapsed in the highlands of central Mexico. Two sites, in particular, stand out: Teotihuacán, the "city of the gods," where one civilization reached its zenith at the time of the Roman empire; and then, a few centuries later, Tula, whose ruins still stand some fifty-six miles northwest of Mexico City.

Around AD 1000 Tula Took Over the Heritage of Teotihuacán

In the eyes of those who live in the central Mexican highlands, the Toltecs of Tula will always remain the unequaled masters of all the material, technical, and intellectual refinements of civilization. They are known as the inventors of painting, sculpture, and the pictographic writing that covered papers of bark or agave with glyphs, the builders of magnificent palaces, and the creators of the mosaics of multicolored feathers that decorated shields and adornments.

The Toltecs worshiped numerous deities, including the god Quetzalcoatl, the Plumed Serpent, whose priest took his name, directed his cult, and governed Tula. The Toltec universe was far from being completely homogeneous: Settled and nomadic peoples lived side by side, and successive waves of immigrants came from the north. Each group maintained its own organization, traditions, and cults.

Many worked the land, but towns were home to the technicians who built the dikes and dams,

Toltec Atlas figure.

which were indispensable to the irrigation of the land. The specialists in the ritual calendar that marked the rhythm of everyone's existence also lived in towns.

In the eyes of the Toltecs the ceremonies conducted by their priests were the only ones that could ensure the continuity of the cosmos and the gods, the return of rain, and the growth of maize.

The domestication of maize occurred several millennia ago in central Mexico. This vital discovery led to the birth of the first agricultural civilizations in the New World.

During the 12th Century the Toltecs Migrated and Dispersed, Their Domination Over

For reasons that remain mysterious, Tula ebbed in power, and the great center of the Toltec period crumbled and then collapsed, toward the middle of the 12th century. Doubtless the Toltecs could absorb no more northerners. The balance between

This part of the *Codex Azcatitlan* depicts the Mexica tribe during the earliest migration. The Mexica crossed mountainous regions occupied by wild beasts, where the vegetation was made up of agaves, rushes, firs, and palm trees.

the settled population and the new arrivals broke down, and migration became the only solution to numerous conflicts.

Camaxtli, the Tlaxcalan god of the north, hunting, and war. He was venerated by the Mexica under the name Mixcoatl.

According to legend, tensions and rivalries forced the priest-king, or the god Quetzalcoatl, or both together—traditions differ on this point—to flee Tula around 1168, accompanied by his followers. Some flooded into the Valley of Mexico (a 70 x 40–mile region to the south, where today's Mexico City is situated), where they helped found new cities, which thus maintained the Toltec heritage. Other migrants reached Cholula, to the south, or even went as far east as Chichén Itzá, where they met the Maya of the Yucatán.

But the inheritors of Toltec culture were not the only people to reach the Valley of Mexico. Nomads or semi-nomads of various ethnic origins came down from the great northern plains and joined them or forced them to share the land. Sometimes, several groups

Statue of Xochipilli, god of flowers, love, dancing, and poetry.

In the *Codex Telleriano-Remensis* the different phases of history are punctuated with calendrical glyphs.

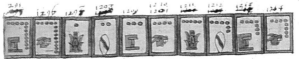

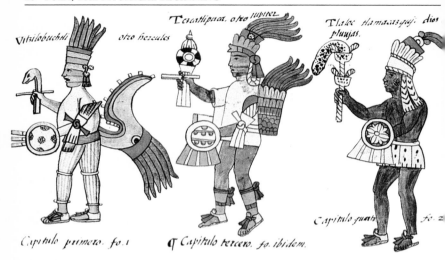

Vitilobuchtli   *otro hercules*   *Tescatlipuca, otro Jupiter.*   *Tlalec Tlamacazqui, dios pluujas.*

Capitulo primero. fo. 1   *Capitulo tercero. fo. ibidem.*   *Capitulo quarto. fo. 2*

formed a federation: This is how the town of Chalco, for example, was founded.

The Toltec Heritage Lived on Through the Reign of the "God-Men," Who Ruled Their Separate Peoples

The memory of Tula, a utopian model, was a heritage as prestigious as it was widespread.

Toward the year 1200 the leaders of these wandering bands considered themselves representatives of their protector-god, to the point of actually merging with him. These "god-men" had bodies charged with the divine energy that enabled the people to continue their progress and attain the goal that the divinity set them. In this troubled time of migration, people appeared at far-flung sites, and the start of their history is blended with a quest for a promised land.

These successive waves of immigration help explain the extreme political fragmentation of central Mexico, where, up to and even beyond the Spanish conquest, there were dozens of tiny domains whose capitals were sometimes only a few miles apart. During the 13th century the nomads became assimilated into what was

Huitzilopochtli, god of war and the sun (above left), was the protector of the Mexica. His name means "hummingbird of the south." Tezcatlipoca, "smoking-mirror," an invisible god (center), was associated with the night and the north. Tláloc, "the germinator" (right), was the god of rain, venerated by peasants. Paynal, a messenger-god (below).

Capitulo segundo.   fo.

left of ancient Toltec culture in the new towns. Many of these were situated around Lake Texcoco, an enormous lake that is now dry.

For Two Centuries Rivalries Arose, Each Town Claiming to Be Descended from the Toltecs

Numerous alliances were made and dissolved between the new centers of power, and these excessively close neighbors constantly fought for supremacy throughout the 13th and 14th centuries.

Culhuacán, south of the lake, had its moment of glory, boasting of being one of the only towns that housed a dynasty of Toltec origin. Later Azcapotzalco, on the western shore, took over this role. The leader of each town tried to link himself with the old Toltec line of descent. For a long time, Toltec—or more exactly Neo-Toltec—was synonymous with nobility, authority, and legitimacy.

"Aztecs," "Mexitin," or "Mexica": A New Group Appeared on the Mexican Scene, Already Well Populated

Toward the beginning of the 13th century a new group whose origins are lost in myth and legend entered the valley. One story goes that this group came from the legendary Chicomóztoc (the "place of seven caves"), a place whose name alludes to their migratory existence at that time. For the Indians, Chicomóztoc was a symbol both of the northern plains that they took so long to cross, and of their original womb.

The group started off by leaving the mysterious Aztlán, a town built on an island. Some believe that the group was called "Aztec" from the very beginning, while others see this name belonging exclusively to the inhabitants of Aztlán in whose power these Toltecs

According to oral tradition, the seven tribes who occupied central Mexico had a common origin. They were said to have come either from a country beyond the sea that surrounds the earth, or from Chicomóztoc, the "place of seven caves." These "seven caves" (illustrated above in a Mexican manuscript) correspond to the seven tribes: the Acolhua, Chalca, Chinampaneca, Culhua, Tepanec, Tlahuica, and Tlatepotzca.

found themselves. Be that as it may, during their migration they were given the name Mexitin and then Mexica. The term "Aztec," which was again adopted in the 18th century, is now generally used to refer to the peoples of the Valley of Mexico, starting in the 15th century.

Huitzilopochtli, God of War and the Sun, Protected the Exodus of the Mexica

Guided by its god Huitzilopochtli, who spoke through the voice of his four bearers, the group undertook a long migration through the north. The history that was reconstructed afterward is preserved in pictographic manuscripts by, among others, the indigenous historian Hernando de Alvarado Tezozómoc. The Mexica practiced agriculture occasionally but lived mostly by hunting. They spoke Nahuatl. In the course of their

travels they underwent splits and disagreements, new bands joined them, and others broke away. Several legendary episodes evoke these wanderings, the outcome of which consolidated Huitzilopochtli's position as the supreme god of the Mexica. The massive executions that were the finale of these events foreshadow the widespread Aztec practice of human sacrifice.

After arriving in the Valley of Mexico, the Mexica found they still lacked leaders of royal stock, and tried in vain to found a permanent settlement. They lived for a while on the western shore of Lake Texcoco, at Chapultepec, where they attracted the hostility of the Tepanec people of Azcapotzalco. Around 1299 they were forced to take refuge to the south of the lake, on the outskirts of Culhuacán.

Here they were offered hospitality on the rocky

According to one version of the migrations, the Mexica crossed Michoacán (southwest Mexico), "land of those who possess fish," before settling at Tenochtitlán (below). Dazzled by this country's beauty, they consulted the god Huitzilopochtli and asked him to allow them to populate it, even though it was not the one he had promised them.

stretches of Tizapan by the Culhua, who hoped that the venomous snakes infesting this area would kill them. No such luck: The Mexica roasted and ate the reptiles. Taking advantage of this break from traveling, which lasted several years, they

began to become "Toltecized."

However, in 1323 they were chased off again. They were forced to penetrate the lake's marshes, where they reached the island that marked the end of their migration.

The Mexica Founded Tenochtitlán, the Site of Modern Mexico City

In 1325 the Mexica discovered the sign they had been waiting for. An eagle perched on a cactus showed them the site where they were to settle: Tenochtitlán. Shortly afterward, a few miles away, they founded the town of Tlatelolco on another island.

Nothing at that time distinguished this hunting-and-gathering people from the other immigrants. Their tiny territory was squashed between the borders of the great domains that dominated the valley.

For thirty years the Mexica led an isolated existence, devoting themselves to building their two towns. Then they applied themselves to creating and developing artificial islands, *chinampas*, floating gardens that, with constant irrigation and much care and attention, produced high yields. But the lack of stone, wood, and other raw materials eventually led the Mexica to emerge from their isolation and establish relations with the outside world.

The eagle on the cactus devouring a snake—the emblem of the founding of Tenochtitlán by the Mexica—is a late development. Sources from before the arrival of the Spanish do not mention the snake, but rather the prickly pear, the fruit that symbolized the heart of sacrificial victims. This image did not escape the Spaniards, who replaced the prickly pear with the snake (an animal more in keeping with the idea of evil) being eaten by the eagle.

The Mexica Chose Acamapichtli, a Lord from the Surrounding Area, as a Leader

Acamapichtli was supposed to be a descendant of the god-priest of Tula, Quetzalcoatl, and in the eyes of the local people he embodied the prestige of the Toltec past. He remained the leader of Tenochtitlán

Despite enormous technical limitations, the Mexica succeeded in carving impressive blocks of stone that they polished with abrasives and used in the construction of pyramids and palaces.

from 1372 to 1391, devoting himself to resisting pressures from nearby Azcapotzalco, the nearby Tepanec town whose power had developed considerably.

The people of the other Mexica town, Tlatelolco, chose a Tepanec prince to lead them. In this way the Mexica managed progressively to insert themselves into the network of alliances that united the valley's centers of power. Furthermore, a dynasty was founded at Tenochtitlán, and the many sons of Acamapichtli were to be the start of a new ruling class dedicated to monopolizing power in Mexica society.

The ruler of Azcapotzalco, a Tepanec called

Tezozómoc, was the region's strongman at the time. Through diplomatic skill and military victories, he had managed to build a true empire. A master at the art of dividing his neighbors by a systematic exploitation of a network of marriage alliances and payment of tribute, he subjugated almost all the region's many towns, creating the most complete domination that central

The *chinampas,* floating gardens, were held in place by stakes and trees planted in the muddy bottom of the lagoon. Opposite: Contemporary drawings of the wildlife in Lake Texcoco.

Mexico had known since the Toltec collapse.

The Mexica gradually became privileged members of Tezozómoc's empire and were even able, with his consent, to extend their territory. Although still confined to secondary roles, they managed to take advantage of this period to train themselves.

Texcoco Was the Only Rival Capable of Countering Tepanec Power

Meanwhile, the northeast region of the Valley of Mexico received a large contingent of nomads, and one of their chiefs made Texcoco—which had been founded at the time of the Toltecs—his capital. Here, as elsewhere, the newcomers knew how to adopt the Toltec heritage: They began speaking Nahuatl, adopted local etiquette, and wore luxurious clothes, while a group of immigrants from the southern region of Oaxaca introduced the arts of goldworking and of pictographic manuscripts.

Gradually Texcoco, the city to which history would give the prestigious title of "Athens of America," became a center of refined civilization. Goldworking, jewelry, the cutting of semiprecious stones, and feather-work mosaics were all such important and respected activities in the Aztec world that even the noblest lords were not above devoting their leisure time to them.

The artisans who worked the precious

This native lord is dressed in the traditional loincloth, the *maxtlatl*, and a cotton cloak, the *tilmatli*.

The Aztec empire was set up in less than a century, emerging from a confused situation in which the whole center of the land was divided into numerous small, independent states. Each of these states had the same governmental structure: A monarch ruled, assisted by one or sometimes several counsels and surrounded by dignitaries entrusted with military or administrative functions. In all cases, the backbone of its domination was the tribute paid to the monarch by the subject towns. The lists of tribute indicated type and quantities, enumerating live birds, precious stones, maize, gold, pimento, clothing, and bales of cotton and woven blankets (left).

metals, stones, and feathers were given the title of "Toltecs," because the invention of these techniques was attributed to the ancient civilization of Tula and its fabled hero, the god-king Quetzalcoatl. They formed corporations that were grouped in their own districts, with their own gods and special rituals.

Tenochtitlán, Texcoco, and Tacuba Formed a Durable Bond in 1428: The Triple Alliance

So it was at the beginning of the 15th century, when Texcoco was starting to assert itself as a power of the first order, that Tezozómoc set out to clinch his domination over the area. War broke out, and in 1418 the leader of Texcoco, Ixtlilxóchitl, had to abandon his city. A large part of Texcocan territory fell under Tepanec rule.

Yet the empire built by Tezozómoc was barely to survive him. One of his sons, Maxtla, succeeded him around 1426. His brutality and errors quickly signaled the end of Tepanec domination.

Gold and silver jewelry was made (above left) using the lost-wax process. The object's form was carved and engraved in charcoal, which served as a mold. The coating of molten gold or silver would ultimately assume the carved shape.

The new leader of Azcapotzalco found Tenochtitlán and Texcoco in league against him. Nezahualcóyotl, Ixtlilxóchitl's legitimate heir, established his authority over Texcoco, and, in 1428, Azcapotzalco fell after a siege lasting 114 days. The Triple Alliance of the Mexica, the Texcocans, and the Tacubans finally succeeded in breaking Tepanec power, and it took control of Tepanec lands.

The essential elements of the political scene that the Spaniards were to discover in 1519 were now in place. The Triple Alliance was to become the "Aztec empire."

The gold jewelry found in a tomb at Monte Albán—the mask of the god Xipe Totec (above) and pectoral (opposite right)—constitutes some of the rare pieces that escaped the Spaniards' greed. The Aztecs' clothing was relatively simple, but their elaborate jewelry was a mark of status.

In 1440 the emperor Moctezuma I, forty years old, came into power. He had met with great success as a warrior, but his greatest victories were before him. In fact, he was to be remembered as the father of the Aztec empire. His reign opened with a series of terrible catastrophes.

CHAPTER II

THE EMPIRE BUILDERS

This calendar (right) became the symbol of the Aztecs, almost on a par with the cactus and the eagle. At the center of the sun stone is a human face with its tongue hanging out, traditionally interpreted as that of Tonatiuh, the sun god, demanding offerings of human blood. Opposite: Tláloc, god of rain.

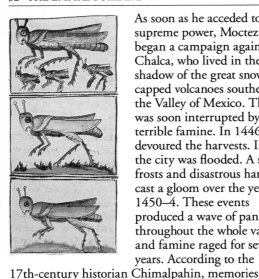

As soon as he acceded to supreme power, Moctezuma I began a campaign against the Chalca, who lived in the shadow of the great snow-capped volcanoes southeast of the Valley of Mexico. This war was soon interrupted by a terrible famine. In 1446 locusts devoured the harvests. In 1449 the city was flooded. A series of frosts and disastrous harvests cast a gloom over the years 1450–4. These events produced a wave of panic throughout the whole valley, and famine raged for several years. According to the 17th-century historian Chimalpahin, memories of vultures circling in the sky were still vivid in people's minds 150 years later. This succession of calamities clearly showed the inadequacies of an authority whose power was based on extremely lax organization.

The chronological system of the ancient Mexicans was founded on the overlapping of a solar calendar of 365 days and a divinatory calendar of 260 days. Each day of the solar calendar was designated by the name of the ritual day corresponding to it. The year always started with one of the four bearer-signs: the reed, the sacrificial knife, the house, or the rabbit. In order to make the two calendars correspond, these four signs were each combined with the thirteen ritual numbers (below), thus giving fifty-two years.

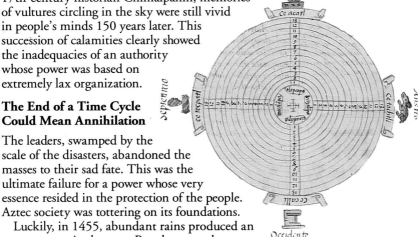

The End of a Time Cycle Could Mean Annihilation

The leaders, swamped by the scale of the disasters, abandoned the masses to their sad fate. This was the ultimate failure for a power whose very essence resided in the protection of the people. Aztec society was tottering on its foundations.

Luckily, in 1455, abundant rains produced an enormous maize harvest. But that year also coincided with the end of a fifty-two–year cycle, a crucial date marked by anxiously performed ceremonies: If, at a specific time, a fire was not relit on the Hill of the Star, the world would disappear.

The Aztecs believed that our universe is extinguishable and that time consists of a chain of cycles ultimately doomed to lead to annihilation. It was said that the twilight monsters, the Tzitzimime, awaited the fatal hour far to the west and would rush to attack the living unless the fires were relit at just the right time. But this time the fires burned again. The earlier disasters were attributed to the gods' anger.

Moctezuma I Decided to Start a Perpetual War With the People of Puebla and Tlaxcala

In order to appease the gods and to capture the largest possible number of prisoners, who were to become

The passage from one fifty-two-year cycle to another was marked by an important ritual. At sunset the priests climbed to the temple at the top of an extinct volcanic crater known as Hill of the Star, and waited for the appearance of the Pleiades. A new fire was lit in the open chest of a victim. Then runners set their torches ablaze and relit the flames in the altars.

fiesta d[e] los niños a los tres dios[es] d[e] la una d[e] la geni[?]
lla y d[e] q[ue] d[e]lic[a]na/ aqui nac[e] nta
mnger

Dios d[e] los niños q[ue]
el q[ue] s[e] g[?]a lleaq[?]
en mis[?] [?]oh[?]g[?]i[?]
d[e] los nt[?]il[?] [?]olacé caial

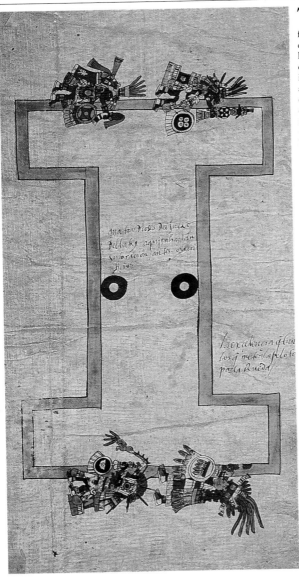

mato dioses pasnear
dabaky aquinhazian
suoracion en los oran
dios

mexicana q bien
los q meten la pelota
pola Rueda

There were two to three hundred festivals per year, a crucial element of indigenous life; they satisfied the desire to integrate the individual into society by all possible means and expressed different ways of conceiving and stabilizing time through the repetition of rituals. The ceremony called *xocotl* (opposite) took place in the tenth month of the year. The people holding hands are captives, dressed in loincloths and paper cloaks. They danced for part of the night and, in the morning, were sacrificed by being burned at the stake in honor of the god Paynal.

The ball game called *tlachtli* (left), is depicted in manuscripts by a double-T shape. Two teams faced each other, and the game consisted of moving a ball into the opponents' area by touching it only with the knees or hips. On the side walls there are two stone rings through which the players had to pass the ball. Like all Aztec games, this one had a symbolic dimension: The court represented the world, and the ball, either the sun or the moon.

sacrificial offerings, regular campaigns were organized. The idea was not so much to conquer the enemy but to find offerings for the gods. These wars were huge ceremonial games, regular training exercises for actual campaigns. They were called the Wars of the Flowers.

They were not a complete innovation; they were probably the systematization of earlier practices known to the ancient Mexicans. Not every war declared by the Aztecs was a War of the Flowers: A conflict's ritual aspects often overlapped with strategic or commercial aims.

The most enviable fate, and the one closest to Aztec vocation, was to die in combat or on a sacrificial stone. By such means one would join the sun in its triumphal march. This belief was the justification for a century of the Wars of the Flowers.

An early Spanish map of Mexico (below) and depictions of human sacrifices.

Be that as it may, from this point on hostilities never ceased to dominate relations between the Triple Alliance and the peoples of the Valley of Puebla and Tlaxcala. They lasted until the arrival of the Spanish (in the 16th century), who took excellent advantage of this particular combination of circumstances.

These hostilities were in keeping with a vigorous renewal of Aztec expansion east and south, toward the rich tropical countries that had taken in the starving refugees from the Valley of Mexico. The lands of the Gulf of Mexico abounded in feathers, precious stones, cotton, and brilliantly colored fabrics. Naturally the valley's nobles coveted all these goods.

Moctezuma I Set Out to Conquer the Tropics

Moctezuma began by striking blows to the southeast, and in 1458 seized Coixtlahuaca, a city famous for its market. The key to the land of the Mixtecs—a land of an ancient civilization renowned for its painted codices and its goldwork—Coixtlahuaca opened up the route to far-off Guatemala.

Moctezuma's invading troops then moved east, toward the Gulf of Mexico, forcing the Huaxtecs and Totonacs to pay tribute. In 1466 a large-scale campaign was carried out against the city of Tepeaca, which commanded the routes leading both south and southeast. The payment of tribute and the careful acquisition of strategic bases on commercial axes all indicate the extent to which economic preoccupations guided the Triple Alliance's military enterprises.

In warfare the Aztecs wore special protective clothing. The warrior's classic armor, *ichcahuipilli* ("cotton bodice"), was a padded vest.

The Triple Alliance's Expansion Was Accompanied by a Reordering of Mexica and Texcocan Society

At both Tenochtitlán and Texcoco, a complex etiquette henceforth marked the life of the sovereign and courtiers. One indicator of the progressive centralization of power was the fact that Moctezuma and his brother Tlacaélel enjoyed extraordinary privileges that distinguished them from the aristocracy. Rank was marked by adornments and clothing whose degree of luxury and refinement varied according to the wearer. Thus, bracelets, brilliant feathers, golden diadems, and greenstones were reserved for the aristocracy. The wearing of cotton garments and the length of mantles were fixed by strict rules; any violation was punished severely.

Although related to a preoccupation with elegance, these rules of clothing were, above all, signs of social status, aimed at differentiating common people from hereditary nobility.

However, it was not a closed system: Warriors who distinguished themselves through bravery also received their share of honors and such adornments as shell

Princes and dignitaries made great use of the sumptuous green feathers of the quetzal and the red and yellow feathers of parrots.

or bone necklaces and eagle feathers. The commoners had to make do with obsidian earrings and rabbit skins.

These differences constituted a crucial feature of Aztec cultures: The conventions went beyond social distinctions, and were aimed at integrating the individual into society, removing any personal particularities by assigning everyone a role, a visual character, and, indeed, a definite image.

It was also in the reign of Moctezuma I and of Nezahualcóyotl, his Texcocan ally, that laws were set up that fixed systematic penalties for adulterers, drunks, and thieves; punishments were especially severe for offenders from the nobility, as if it were not permitted for those in power to set a bad example. Other measures were aimed at guaranteeing the integrity of judges. But these decisions only affected those from the regions of Tenochtitlán and Texcoco.

Featherwork, reserved for plumage specialists, was carried out as follows: A framework of reeds was covered with a screen of fairly ordinary feathers to make a solid base. The featherworkers always used the same method of fixing them in place. They would reinforce the feathers' stems with thin bamboo tubes, and then the feathers were fastened in little clusters using agave thread. The whole thing was fixed to the framework with a thicker thread. When this screen was in place, the same process was carried out with the precious feathers (quetzal, macaw, and so on)—their stems were consolidated, and they were basted before being sewn to the framework. The white down of the quetzal feathers (which were a golden green) was concealed with a fringe of pink-colored feathers, which was then set in place on top.

The Triple Alliance's Military Expeditions Displayed Weakness As Well As Strength

The establishment of Aztec rule in far-off lands was not a foregone conclusion: The Aztecs left no garrison behind, except for an official whose job was to collect tribute and to make sure it was sent to Tenochtitlán. Apart from this, the Mexica and their allies respected local authorities, institutions, and traditions. In any case, they had no regular army, apart from a military elite who were too few in number to serve as an occupying force.

Although the Mexica sometimes imposed the cult of Huitzilopochtli, their tutelary god, they never bothered to proscribe the local divinities. The very idea of

The sacrificed prisoner was no longer an enemy being killed but a messenger being sent to the gods, himself invested with an almost divine dignity. When a man took a prisoner, he said: "Here is my beloved son," and the captive said: "Here is my revered father."

conversion, one of the linchpins of Christianity, was alien to the peoples of Mexico.

Obstacles to True Control: Enormous Distances and Rudimentary Means of Communication

The troops of Tenochtitlán and the caravans bearing tribute had to cover several hundred miles, cross mountains, tackle almost impenetrable vegetation, or traverse cold and dry plateaus, before descending the tropical slopes that led to the Gulf or the Pacific. The difficulties they faced were all the greater in that none of these societies was familiar with the mule, the horse, or the wheel: Everything had to be carried on a human back.

It is therefore easy to understand why the local authorities were sometimes tempted to shake off Aztec control and, in a moment of exasperation, do something irrevocable. However, these spasmodic revolts only resulted in unleashing brutal reprisals, which usually ended in the rebels being crushed and then subjected to even higher payments of tribute.

One of the emperor's primary functions was to command the armies of not only Tenochtitlán but also the allied cities. The great dignitaries surrounding him held offices that were, at least in origin, of a military nature.

Drawings from Diego Durán, *The History of the Indies of New Spain,* 16th century.

The Power of the Triple Alliance Rested on the Image It Created for Itself

The Triple Alliance's carefully nurtured image was both that of a repressive power, founded on armed violence, and that of a more subtle authority, relying on negotiation as much as on terror.

Thus, leaders who had not yet been subjugated by the Triple Alliance were periodically invited to attend the human sacrifices carried out in Tenochtitlán. Received in the greatest luxury, they could observe at leisure the way in which the victims—often their kinspeople, captured in war—were offered to the gods of Tenochtitlán. It was out of the question to turn down the invitation, since any refusal would immediately be seen as a reason for starting war.

The Triple Alliance also knew how to take care of the collaboration of the satellite populations of the Valley of Mexico and its surroundings: In exchange for contingents of warriors, the Aztecs granted them shares in the war booty. Remote cities received preferential treatment, aimed at guaranteeing their loyalty. Others were entrusted with guarding the frontiers, which exempted them from tribute payments.

This empire thus resembled an immense spiderweb, with the Triple Alliance at its center and a thousand networks linked through marriage alliances, exchange of services, interdependence, and extortion. The whole structure was quite flexible and always perfectly adapted to an authority that could rely neither on efficient means of transport nor on alphabetical writing, that instrument of rapid communication. In other words, it was nothing like a highly centralized and totalitarian power.

The Empire Was Far from Being Subject to the Rule of Tenochtitlán Alone. Texcoco, Its Partner in the Triple Alliance, Was No Mere Second Best

Texcoco received the same share of tribute as Tenochtitlán, that is, two-fifths. It took part in the

Every man in Tenochtitlán was a warrior. Only when he had captured prisoners could he reach the upper ranks and wear feather headdresses and leather bracelets.

military campaigns, extended its hold over neighboring towns and the northeastern part of the valley, and received tribute from the lands of the Gulf of Mexico.

Moreover, Texcoco exercised remarkable cultural influence, due to the activities of Texcoco's Nezahualcóyotl, a particularly brilliant ruler. Renowned as a legislator—he revived some laws of Quetzalcoatl, his Toltec ancestor—builder, and poet, Nezahualcóyotl had the allure of a renaissance prince.

At the end of his career a warrior could attain one of the two upper military orders: that of the "jaguar-knight," whose war costume was a jaguar skin, and that of the "eagle-knight," whose helmet was an eagle head.

He was said to be descended from the gods and to be immortal, qualities lacking in his ally Moctezuma. According to one of his descendants, the chronicler Alva Ixtlilxóchitl, he even had the intuition of a supreme god, creator of heaven and earth; Ixtlilxóchitl enthusiastically called him "the most powerful, valiant, and wise prince…there has ever been in this New World."

Nezahualcóyotl (below, 1402–72), king of Texcoco, a poet, philosopher, and talented builder, was the most refined representative of Mexican culture.

Payment of Tribute Formed the Backbone of the Empire

Brought in by endless lines of bearers converging on the Aztec capital, tribute represented everything ancient Mexico could produce and consume. Several tens of thousands of tons of food, more than 100,000 cotton garments, over 30,000 bundles of feathers, and an impressive quantity of precious objects and rare animals constituted the tribute paid in a year.

Supervised by local tax collectors at the point of departure, the tribute was carefully counted. Evidence of this can be found in several codices.

The merchandise

had many destinations: In a society that did not distinguish between work and religious rites, and in which there was a whole series of ceremonies and rituals throughout the year, part of the tribute was used to provide these feast days with their usual ostentation.

Another part was devoted to administration, the citizens' subsistence, and the costs of war. Another was put back into circulation by means of the powerful merchants of Tlatelolco, who traded it for other goods.

To the tribute were added the teams of workers the subject populations were required to provide Tenochtitlán. These multitudes of laborers took part in the great construction projects in the capital.

In 1465 Moctezuma undertook a huge campaign and managed to conquer Chalco after twenty years of hostilities. He died shortly afterward, in 1469. He had been the tireless architect of Aztec power.

The objects of tribute depicted above include (lower right) two lots of four hundred bales of dried pimento and a headdress of quetzal feathers.

In 1472, shortly after Moctezuma's death, his great ally, the poet-king Nezahualcóyotl, died in his turn. The Triple Alliance, increasingly powerful, passed to a series of rulers who extended the limits of the Aztec empire through a combination of warfare and diplomacy.

CHAPTER III
THE AZTECS, CONQUERING HEROES

The sight of human blood on the 114 steps (opposite) of one of the two sanctuaries of the Great Temple of Tenochtitlán horrified the Spaniards who had just arrived in Mexico. Right: 17th-century view of Mexico City.

The most serious crisis erupted in 1473 when Tlatelolco, the commercial capital of the Mexica, rose up against its immediate neighbor and twin city, Tenochtitlán. There is little doubt that Tlatelolco, which had obtained considerable wealth from the booty of previous conquests, tolerated its secondary status less and less.

It had cause for regret. Axayácatl, Moctezuma's successor, emerged victorious from the confrontation, sacked the city, and proceeded to deprive Tlatelolco of its autonomy.

However, Tlatelolco was not crushed. Until the Spanish conquest, it continued to house an extremely active population of merchants who visited the whole of Mexico. It also kept its great market, the marvels and riches of which were listed admiringly by the conquistadors half a century later: gold, silver, precious stones, slaves, cacao, ocelot and deer hides, game, tobacco, and herbs, to name but a few.

Axayácatl repeatedly led campaigns to the west and northwest. However, these sorties continually ended in failure: The Tarascans of Michoacán proved to be tough combatants. Axayácatl's successor, Tízoc, scarcely fared any better and died quite soon after taking power.

Axayácatl, whose reign lasted from 1469 to 1481, strengthened the Aztec empire.

A Sovereign Worthy of the Empire: Ahuítzotl, the Warrior

Ahuítzotl came to power in 1486 and began by leading several campaigns against provinces in revolt: They provided him with the captives required by his priests, since the work on the Great Temple of Tenochtitlán, begun under Moctezuma I, was nearing completion.

The inauguration of this monument was the occasion for splendid feasts, as well as a tremendous holocaust. Some sources quote the terrible figure of 80,400 victims sacrificed in four days. Although this is probably an exaggeration, it nevertheless seems probable that several thousand men and women were sacrificed to the gods of Tenochtitlán in 1487. Immense lines of captives prepared for death converged from the north, east, south, and west on the capital's ceremonial center.

In ancient Mexico, human sacrifice (top) was an offering to the gods of people's most precious possession, their blood. The custom that most startled the Spaniards, ritual cannibalism (above), was in fact the attainment of a spiritual idea: It was a true communion.

CARTE DU MEXIQUE

GOLFE DU CANCRE

MEXIQUE

MER PACIFIQUE

Midy

Quincla — Xacus — Saleus — Tammanpul — Tanapequi — Nort — Tanxiro — Tampico — San — Xacano — Tamaco — Hermose — Salina — R. de Palmas

Tropique

St. Filippe — Tamaolen — delos Xauor — P. Loco — Panuco — Tamaliae — Tempice — Rexo — Salines

Guoxanato — Tampara — Tazatlan — Xasiquohud — Sauquibtla — I. Lobes — Ichtopaxapan — P. Casenes

St. Miguel — Concesion — de Salaia — Puchuca — Achichica — S. Pedra — MEXIQUE

Villa de Solagos — Xasnehtitla — Ilacorign — Cacatlan — Cacere — Tlanos — Neotlan — de Almeria — Toluca — Almeria — Terrebiance

Xacot de la — MEXICO — Talula — Tlascala — Villavera — Zulcneque

Vol atco — Gua socena — Cholula — Temba — Matatlan — Teuancapola — I. de Sacrificios

Talista — Guernaba — Tepeaca — Salaio — Veracrux — S. Ingadulia — ostuma — Tentales — Zecetlan

Quecala — Chiuatla — Chisnantla — Rio S. Pedra

Chaxalcte — Pucla — Antequera

Hutatlan — Cata — Wutla — P. dos Yores — Csasila — Tatepeque — Aqautulco

Acapulco — Tuxuluta — capala — Tecapteque

a de plus dans ce
blie à Mexique, on
idiës dans toutes
ni il y a des Com

Ce grand Temple des Mexicains etoit consacré à l'Idole Vitzilipuztli c'est à dire le Dieu de la Guerre, & le Souve-
rain de tous leurs autres Dieux. Pour y arriver on entroit d'abord dans une grande place quarrée formée
de murailles, ou plusieurs couleurs de relief entrelassées de diverses manieres imprimoient de l'hor-
reur, sur tout au frontispice de la premiere porte qui en etoit chargé. On rencontroit auparavant une espece

La pla
fiers etoie
bituma re
ou l'escala

Dances appellées Mitoles.

Idole de Vitztzili

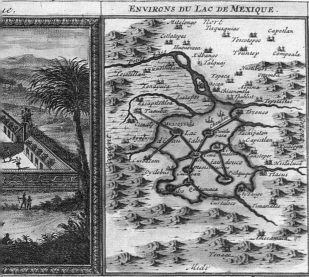

ENVIRONS DU LAC DE MEXIQUE.

Nort

Mitalongo Tisquiquiac Capotlan
Cillatopee Tescotopee
Huouocea Touutep Compoala
Xilbango Talguaj
Teotihtlan Nuxbaic Ottemba
Tepeca
Tenayuca Tocan Chiconotla Azluma
Escapitzalco Tepotzotlac
Tlauba Esalope Tezcuco
Climalt Mexiquett Pacalpaton Capistlan
Atoluta Lac Poula Ataloa Talocpa
d'Eau Salee vaca
Cuiboleam Cima valle faut douce Nilaluca
magna vaca Pichquipu Tlacus
Villobus Calhuan
Mo Quilguaca Ixtango Timanales
Curtalece Timanaltes
Amecamaca
Tenaae
Midy

On arriving in Tenochtitlán, the Spaniards were deeply impressed by the beauty, order, and cleanliness of this city of between 150,000 and 300,000 inhabitants, one of the biggest metropolises in the world at the time. But this favorable impression rapidly vanished when they reached the great ceremonial center. The immense enclosure, measuring 1320 x 1000 feet, contained several dozen temples, the highest and largest of which was the Great Temple. While experiencing the visual shock of seeing the blood-soaked steps leading to the sanctuary of Huitzilopochtli, the Spaniards were struck by its terrible smell. These are French engravings from the end of the 17th century.

La Ville de Mexique.

Ahuítzotl himself, the sovereign, struck the first blow, surrounded by the leaders of Texcoco and Tacuba at the top of the Great Temple. When they tired of opening chests and pulling out the victims' still-beating hearts, dozens of priests took over from them in this endless, gigantic massacre.

It was a grandiose spectacle. In the flower-bedecked temples there was nonstop singing and dancing; sacrificers and victims wore the sumptuous adornments of the gods whose presence on earth they thus demonstrated. Blood flowed down the walls and the pyramid steps. It is not difficult to imagine what an unbearable stench must have been produced by these sacrifices. Alva Ixtlilxóchitl, the chronicler, wrote a century after the Spanish conquest: "This butchery remains unequaled in history."

The Aztecs Did Not Invent Human Sacrifice; It Had Been Practiced at Teotihuacán a Millennium Earlier

How are we to make sense of this extraordinary scene and the killings, which were planned down to the last detail? The Aztecs sacrificed their victims on an unprecedented scale and appear to have been obsessed by the urgency of carrying out mass human sacrifices. They were motivated by many factors.

By far the most important concerned their gods and the cosmos. The Aztec gods were mortal, so they had a constant need to be fed. Once fed, they would ensure that the rains returned regularly, make sure the soils were fertile, and help the sun in its daily journey. If the gods were not fed, the world would come to an end.

In addition, human sacrifice was an instrument of government, upholding a policy of terror and at the same time enabling the physical elimination of the most dangerous conquered people, that is, leaders and warriors. In a way, ancient Mexican societies were "societies of spectacle," with power exhibited not so much

"It was forbidden only to kill the chiefs.... The lord prisoner climbed up there, and a long thin rope was attached to his instep. He was given a sword and a roundel, and the one who had captured him came to fight him.**"**
Narrative of the Anonymous Conquistador, c.1530

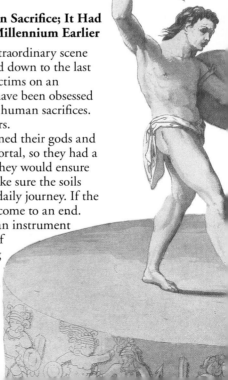

through a complex bureaucracy as through gigantic displays of the victors' inexorable greatness.

The Grandiose Staging of Sacrifices Was the Reflection of the Cosmos on Earth

These countless killings constituted the source of vital energy, of "precious water"—that is, of blood—that was indispensable for the working of the cosmos. That effort had constantly to be renewed through colossal, minutely controlled rituals.

On these occasions, both priests and victims took on the gods' features. Indeed, they became the gods, man and god uniting, in order to allow divine power to manifest itself before the fascinated gaze of the crowds. The sacrificial victim was more than an enemy being killed.

Today perhaps, in a world where image and

"He was cut up; one of his thighs was sent for Moctezuma's meal, and the rest was divided between the people of rank or relatives. They normally went to the house of whoever had brought the dead man into captivity. This flesh was cooked with maize."
Bernardino de Sahagún,
*Florentine Codex:
General History of the
Things of New Spain,*
16th century

reality are becoming interchangeable, we may be better able to understand those societies that gathered all their resources to create a spectacle for themselves, in order to exist, to acquire a profound identity, and to delay the final cataclysm.

The annihilation of vast numbers of human lives was, in its own way, a form of conspicuous consumption aimed at impressing subject peoples and neighbors.

The same unbridled lavishness, one of the essential aspects of the ceremonies, was also on display during the banquets sponsored by rich merchants. A whole year's tribute was spent, or rather, invested in this way for the grandiose coronation feasts of emperor Ahuítzotl in 1486.

War, Tribute, and Human Sacrifice Linked the Government to the Regeneration of the Cosmos

The dual necessity of reinforcing the Triple Alliance's domination and of ceaselessly renewing the food of the

The priests threw the victim down on the sacrificial stone, opened the chest with a flint knife, and pulled out the heart, which was then burned in a stone urn. The victim wore the clothing of the god and was called *ixiptla,* "the god's image." Above: Drawing from an Aztec codex. Right: A 19th-century depiction. Left: The sacrificial knife was a piece of quartz in the form of a spear point.

gods led Ahuítzotl to adopt a policy of nonstop expansion. Campaigns were restarted and intensified, first to the south, toward the hot countries leading down to the Pacific.

Colonies of Indians from Tenochtitlán were even settled in the south, their mission being to develop plantations of cacao, a luxury commodity reserved for the nobility, and to keep guard over the border with their dangerous Tarascan neighbors. The ruler of Texcoco, the wise Nezahualpilli, son of Nezahualcóyotl, helped this enterprise with his advice, but from this time on it became clear that Tenochtitlán took the upper hand in the military affairs of the Triple Alliance.

A *teocalli*, a type of Aztec temple (below).

"[The city's] form is square and resembles a chessboard because of its straight, wide, and well-paved streets which correspond to the four principal winds."
Giovanni Francesco Gemelli-Careri,
A Voyage Around the World, 1719

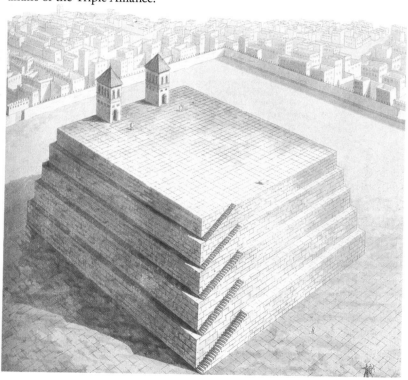

Just as Christopher Columbus Was Landing in the West Indies, Ahuítzotl Reached Acapulco

Pushing on with his expansion, Ahuítzotl occupied the shores of the Pacific between 1491 and 1495. The conquest of the province of Oaxaca, begun under Moctezuma I, brought into Mexico a flood of rich tribute in gold, cochineal, and painted cotton.

Further south, the Zapotec town of Tehuantepec became the Aztecs' goal. In order to capture this important trading center, they set off on their longest expedition, causing unprecedented problems in logistics, administration, and troop coordination.

In 1500 Tehuantepec asked for the aid of Ahuítzotl against Soconusco, near the present-day Guatemalan border, about six hundred miles southeast of Mexico City. This was to be a very difficult campaign: Not only did it require enormous resources to provide for the troops' subsistence over such a great distance, but the rulers of Tacuba and Texcoco came up with excuses for not joining Ahuítzotl. So he alone became head of the armies, and alone he conquered Soconusco.

However, Mexica expansion ended here, because the Triple Alliance's armies were fighting on several fronts at once (against the domains of the Valley of Puebla, Huejotzingo, and Tlaxcala). There is every reason to believe that some of these victories were precarious.

Chronicle showing the reign of Ahuítzotl.

While Ahuítzotl Was Constantly Pushing Back the Empire's Borders, the Valley of Mexico Prospered

In order to tackle the problems associated with an increasing population, remarkable engineering projects were achieved at Tenochtitlán. This island city, built up along canals, was connected to the mainland by causeways, protected from flooding by dikes, and supplied with fresh water by aqueducts. But in 1503 a flood destroyed the capital's houses and gardens, which then were abandoned by the nobility.

Ahuítzotl was forced to turn to his Texcoco ally for guidance. Nezahualpilli suggested that he appease the gods by celebrating various rites. The strategist yielded to the sage's advice. The waters subsided. It was decided to reconstruct the city.

Teams of workers sent by the cities in the valley were shared by the noble families who made them construct elegant, brightly painted palaces with splendid gardens and patios. Along the canal banks willows and poplars were planted; dikes were strengthened. The capital, Tenochtitlán, took on a whole new appearance, reflecting the empire's wealth and greatness. It was this new city that was to fill Cortés' troops with wonder when they discovered it almost twenty years later.

The flood served to reveal the tensions caused within the Triple Alliance by the power of the Mexica. Ahuítzotl ordered the assassination of a lord who had seen fit to advise against the water conveyance project, and this cold-blooded murder spread fear and confusion in the Valley of Mexico. Nezahualpilli took advantage of the catastrophe to demonstrate his power to Ahuítzotl.

Nezahualpilli Secured the Influence of Texcoco With the Same Talent as His Father

Thanks to Nezahualpilli's wisdom, diplomacy, and political skill, Texcoco retained an enviable role in the Triple Alliance. Like his father, Nezahualpilli possessed immense knowledge and remarkable gifts: He is supposed to have prophesied the arrival of the "sons of the sun" (the Spaniards) and, according to some, to have escaped death forever by withdrawing to a mysterious cave.

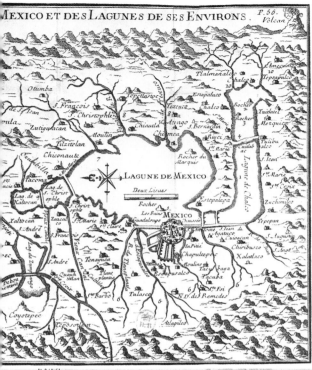

MEXICO ET DES LAGUNES DE SES ENVIRONS.

At the time of the Spanish conquest, the town of Mexico included both Tenochtitlán and Tlatelolco. It stretched from north to south, the northern limit being Tlatelolco, opposite the lakeshore village of Tepeyac. A series of towns marked the southern limit of the urban area: Toltenco ("beside the rushes"), Acatlán ("place of reeds"), Xihuitonco ("meadow"), Atizapan ("whitish water"), Tepetitlan ("beside the hill"), Amanalco ("sheet of water"). To the west it ended in Atlampa ("beside the water") and at Chichimecapan ("the river of the Chichimecs"). In the east it stretched as far as Atlixco ("on the water's surface"), where the open water of Lake Texcoco began. Overall it covered almost four square miles.

Domestic history, however, relates that he had a fairly uneasy private life. He had his principal wife executed, and the same fate befell two of his sons when their conduct displeased him. He kept two thousand concubines, who bore him 144 children. He particularly loved one of the concubines, a noblewoman from Tula, being charmed by her learning and culture. Among the Aztecs, polygamy was the privilege of nobility, but among royalty it took on proportions that seemed to justify the sovereign's almost divine nature.

The Empire's Size Began to Cause Problems

Limits had to be placed on expansion since the Triple Alliance was based on the loyalty and goodwill of local leaders. While the alliance moved into and overtook some neighboring lands, it by no means controlled the conquered countries, owing to lack of both means and men.

Since little integration of foreign populations took place, there was a constant risk of rebellion. The riches accumulated through conquest seemed to lead to a vicious circle. By stimulating the development of the valley and its population, they caused an increase in demands and needs.

However, there is no doubt that the solidity of imperial power depended largely on the way in which the Triple Alliance's nobles and allies took part in the

"We have already mentioned several times that the king of Texcoco, Nezahualpilli [below], had a reputation as a sorcerer or magician, and the most convincing opinion that I have found among the Indians is that he had concluded a pact with the devil."
Diego Durán,
The History of the Indies of New Spain, 16th century

redistribution of tribute. In order to satisfy the needs of the system, it was continually necessary to launch new expeditions, each time to more distant places, making them increasingly dangerous and costly to mount.

In 1503 Moctezuma II Succeeded Ahuítzotl. Under His Reign, Power Became Resolutely Absolute, and the Aztecs Unleashed Hostilities in a More Systematic Fashion

Moctezuma II is the best known of the Aztec rulers. A scrupulous observer of omens and rituals, he was extremely religious, a trait matched in its intensity only by his love of power.

Moctezuma II began by taking radical steps to change the way his ministers were recruited. The officials Ahuítzotl had set in place were eliminated and replaced by a select band of young people, all from the best families. So the nobility's monopoly on power was strengthened, and etiquette around the sovereign became much stricter.

Under Moctezuma II, the Aztec system was changed from a crude democracy to one of absolute power, in which class privileges predominated. It was possibly due to these measures that the military and clerics reacted against the constantly growing influence of the great merchants, who flourished after the Triple Alliance's territorial expansion.

As for the outside world, Moctezuma II was to devote the bulk of his forces to subjugating and controlling unconquered pockets of land. Within the Triple Alliance's networks of cities and of peoples, his predecessors' expeditions of conquest or punitive raids had often left gaps, sometimes even whole countries that had escaped paying tribute. The task was now to subjugate and absorb them.

Moctezuma II launched campaigns to the south and the Pacific to subjugate the Yopis in the province of Oaxaca and to conquer the principality of Tututepec—a Mixtec domain in the ancient past. They

The days of the divinatory calendar were designated by twenty signs: aquatic monster, wind, house, lizard, serpent, death, roe deer, rabbit, water, dog, monkey, grass, reed, jaguar, eagle, vulture, earthquake, flint, rain, and flower. These signs always followed each other in the same order. Each of them was accompanied by a number from one to thirteen.

also marched north to finish off Metztitlan.

Tututepec resisted some of the Aztec attacks but the Yopis were conquered, and Metztitlan lost some important positions. Hence new cities located in the Gulf region had to offer tribute to the Triple Alliance.

Moctezuma II renewed his commitment to strengthen his grip on the province of Oaxaca, taking several towns by storm and massacring whole populations. He decided to take these measures both to remove certain bastions that were thought to have become too autonomous and also to eliminate cities that were interfering with the flow of tribute toward Tenochtitlán.

The Aztecs, More Determined than Ever, Abandoned the Ideal of the War of the Flowers

In order to crush their longtime enemies beyond the volcanoes, Moctezuma put an end to the ritualized and balanced exchange of the War of the Flowers. For a long time, the cities of Tlaxcala and Huejotzingo had been surrounded, cut off from the resources afforded by trade and access to the tropical countries of the Gulf of Mexico.

Salt, for example, was cruelly lacking in Tlaxcala, and the natives had to find and eat substitutes for this precious commodity.

Cacao, gold, and feathers were equally rare. Since the reign of Moctezuma I, the campaigns against Huejotzingo and Tlaxcala had become more systematic, but could not really be called all-out war.

In 1504, however, Moctezuma II unleashed hostilities. Taking advantage of a dispute, he waged

MOCTEZUMA XOCOTZIN.

Premier Empereur du Mexique, peint par ordre de Fernand Cortez.

From the start of his reign (1503–20), Moctezuma II undertook to consolidate the empire.

war on Huejotzingo between 1508 and 1513 and on Tlaxcala in 1515. But he suffered some stinging defeats and, at the time of the Spaniards' arrival, the results of his campaigns in the region were poor. The Aztec war machine, so formidable in its distant expeditions, ran aground against Tlaxcalan resistance. A few years later, Cortés would make full use of that unexpected ally's forces.

Thus, before the conquistadors' arrival, the Triple Alliance's influence encompassed almost 78,000 square miles and several million people. The population grew enormously—a dozen cities had more than 10,000 inhabitants, while Tenochtitlán had over 150,000, and may even have reached 300,000.

The organization of government: Power belonged to the *tlatoani* (the emperor), "he who speaks." The *ciuacoatl* organized military expeditions. The four dignitaries including the *tlacatecatl* ("he who commands the warriors") and the *tlacochcalcatl* ("the official of the house of javelins") were elected.

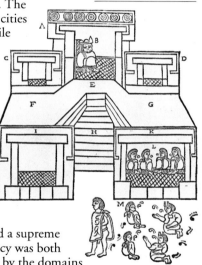

Great Tenochtitlán, Center of the Mexica-Dominated World, Focus of Cosmic Order, Was Ancient Tula Reborn

It was therefore not surprising that, when they saw this unknown, marvelous city, the conquistadors compared it to Venice or the enchanted cities of romantic tales.

Although the Mexica undeniably held a supreme position in Tenochtitlán, their supremacy was both contested and recent. It was challenged by the domains of the Valley of Puebla; and it was recent because it was only in the years 1504–16 that it spectacularly established its position.

Despite this tendency toward centralization, the local dynasties remained in place everywhere, and no imperial administration supplanted them. Numerous, often tiny domains continued to function, and they constituted the foundations on which the Triple Alliance's domination rested.

The local dynasties were closely linked to each other and to Tenochtitlán through marriages, and they

The throne of Moctezuma is depicted above (top) in an early drawing.

White Maize, Black Beans

"And all food necessary to them also was sold separately: dried grains of maize, white, black, red, and yellow; pinto beans; large beans; gray amaranth seed, red amaranth seed, and fish amaranth; white chía, black chía, and the wrinkled variety; salt; fowl; turkey cocks and hens; quail; rabbits, hares, and deer; ducks and other water birds, gulls and wild geese; maguey syrup and honey...."

Bernardino de Sahagún,
*Florentine Codex:
General History of the
Things of New Spain,*
16th century

Fresco by Diego Rivera, *Great Tenochtitlán: The Sale of Maize* (detail), 1945.

Gold, Silver, and Feathers

"The ruler took care of the directing of the marketplace and all things sold, for the good of the common folk, the vassals, and all dwellers in the city, the poor, the unfortunate, so that [these] might not be abused, not suffer harm, not be deceived not disdained. Thus were things bought, or sold: They arranged them in order so that each thing sold would be placed separately—in its own place or station. They were not spread about in confusion. Marketplace directors were appointed to office. They cared for, and attended to, the marketplace and all and each of the things sold —the merchandise which was there. Each of the directors took care, and was charged, that no one might deceive another, and how [articles] might be priced and sold."

Bernardino de Sahagún, *Florentine Codex: General History of the Things of New Spain,* 16th century

Fresco by Diego Rivera, *The Market of Tenochtitlán: Manufacture of Mosaic and Golden Jewelry Under the Zapotec Civilization,* 1942.

frequently received a share of tribute. It was like a sort of profit sharing in the smooth running of the empire.

Under these conditions, the Triple Alliance's survival depended on the loyalty of a few dozen princes who, more or less voluntarily, made regular visits to Tenochtitlán, where they received sumptuous gifts.

The political situation sheds light on the powerful alliance's collapse and the sudden changes in public opinion that took place in the cities when the Spanish arrived.

When Cortés saw Tenochtitlán (above) he said: "The city is so big and so remarkable...larger than Granada and very much stronger, with as good buildings and many more people than Granada had when it was taken."

Hernán Cortés
Letters from Mexico
1519–26

A few rebellions occasionally broke out, like that of Cuetlaxtlán, where the inhabitants, annoyed at having to pay tribute, locked the Aztec tax collectors in a house and set fire to it.

However, the leaders were rarely dismissed, and were accustomed to a large degree of autonomy, and so they came to accept the rule of the Spanish monarchy without realizing the radical upheavals it would eventually bring.

In the first decade of the 16th century, the emperor Moctezuma II thought he had become the "master of the world." But his sovereignty remained precarious. Moctezuma was fated to bow before a bearded white man: Hernán Cortés.

CHAPTER IV

THE CLASH OF TWO WORLDS

"[Cortés'] face, mournful and almost ashy in color, would have been more elegant if it had been longer. The look in his eye was gentle and solemn; his thin, dark beard covered little of his face; his hair, of the same color, had the cut of the period. He was broad-chested and had well-shaped shoulders. He had a slender body, with a little stomach and well-turned legs and thighs."
Bernal Díaz del Castillo,
The Conquest of New Spain,
16th century

The ancient Mexican Indians had a cyclical conception of time. The time of the gods dominated that of humans, and at regular intervals divine forces left their imprint on human existence. Thus, certain conjunctions of forces, coming together in the same way each time, and certain past events were repeated whenever the same divine influences coincided.
In this way it was possible to predict the future, a task that was the privilege of specialized priests who checked the calendar-codices. Careful interpretation of wonders, visions, and dreams could produce particularly valuable information.

"Ten years before the Spaniards came, an evil omen first appeared in the heavens. It was like a tongue of fire, like a flame, like the light of dawn. It seemed to rain down in small droplets, as if it were piercing the sky."
    Bernardino de Sahagún,
    *Florentine Codex:
    General History of the
    Things of New Spain,*
    16th century

Growing Anxieties

The ancient Mexicans were extremely preoccupied with the day-to-day emergence of malevolent nonhuman forces looming outside the ritualized framework of the relationship between humans and gods. In this respect, the decade before the Spaniards' arrival produced plenty of reasons to be fearful. Ten years before Cortés a dazzling comet appeared. The soothsayers proved incapable of interpreting this phenomenon. Moctezuma condemned them to death. Nezahualpilli, who possessed the gift of second sight, prophesied calamities that were to destroy the kingdoms. When he died in 1516, he left behind a perplexed and troubled Moctezuma.

Other marvels came and sowed the seeds of anxiety in the Aztec ruler's mind. One goddess' sanctuary caught fire. The lake's water formed gigantic waves, despite the fact that there was no wind. Women's voices in the night announced death and destruction. An enormous stone began to speak, proclaimed the fall of Moctezuma, and defied attempts to transport it to Tenochtitlán.

The bewildered sovereign thought at one point of committing suicide. At the last minute he was prevented from doing so by his entourage. Plunged into

Below: The god Cipactonal (left) and his wife, Oxomoco, in a cave, are busy devising the divinatory calendar, the *tonalamatl*. This picture is taken from the *Codex Borbonicus*, known as one of the most perfect Aztec codices, both for its content (the Aztec calendar, including depictions of the ritual feast day celebrations) and for the quality of its paintings and their condition.

a state of extreme agitation, Moctezuma demanded to know the dreams and visions of all his subjects, in order to obtain the explanation of the signs and prophecies that were tormenting him.

These wonders may simply demonstrate challenges to a still poorly consolidated authority, as well as the exasperation of a subjugated people.

The Presence of Spaniards Increased the Anxiety Provoked by Gloomy Prophecies

It is difficult to believe that the Spaniards passed completely unnoticed by the Aztecs, having landed in 1492 in the West Indies, settled in Hispaniola and Cuba, and then established themselves on the coasts of Venezuela and Panama. For twenty years European fleets had been cruising between the islands and part of the continent and, when shipwrecks occurred, Indian canoes and Spanish ships spotted each other.

In 1517 a first Spanish expedition touched the eastern coasts of Mexico, in the Yucatán and the Campeche regions. Soon a second expedition left Cuba, reached the island of Cozumel and moved up the Gulf of Mexico as far as Veracruz, before stopping at the mouth of the Pánuco River. There was trading, fighting, and mutual observation.

The new arrivals were very strange, and the Indians wondered about the reason for this sudden invasion. It was reported to Moctezuma that a mountain was moving around on the waters of the Gulf—a Spanish ship had been seen. The question was whether this was the prophesied return of the god Quetzalcoatl and his companions: Tula had collapsed with the departure of Quetzalcoatl, the Plumed Serpent, but the god-priest was due to return in time from the distant east, in accordance with the pattern of cyclical repetition. The conquering shadow of the Toltecs made its last appearance. Ironically, this image, which had never lost its power, loomed up again at the very time when people coming from the east were preparing to

"Nezahualpilli spoke to Moctezuma in a dream as follows, showing him the future portents: 'I must inform you of strange and marvelous things which must come about during your reign. "
Diego Durán,
The History of the Indies of New Spain,
16th century

Signs of the divinatory calendar (below). Specialized priests interpreted the signs and numbers for all circumstances like birth, marriage, the departure of merchants for far-off lands, and the election of chiefs.

overwhelm the Aztecs. Thus history's trap was sprung: How could one try to retain a power inherited from Quetzalcoatl, if the god himself returned to reclaim it?

In 1519 an Expedition Left Cuba to Explore the Coasts of Mexico. At Its Head Was a Thirty-Three-Year-Old Spanish Gentleman, Hernán Cortés

For several years already Moctezuma had been placing lookouts along the shores, to watch for the return of those who were perhaps gods guided by Quetzalcoatl. He knew from legend that the Plumed Serpent would

Yepenqvaoyotl
ycha mote
cinco
m á

Battle between
Spaniards
and Aztecs (left).

This headdress of
green feathers
(below) is mentioned in
the long list of treasures
that Cortés received from
Moctezuma and sent
to Charles V in July
1519; Charles gave it to
his nephew as a gift.

kill the worshipers of Huitzilopochtli. At all costs it
was vital to keep away the white men whose
arrival from the eastern seas could only
announce Quetzalcoatl's return. Would
not the best method be to make them
offerings suited to the god they
represented?

   When he learned in April
1519 that ships had berthed
not far from what was to
become the port of
Veracruz, Moctezuma
had the strangers'
supplies replenished
and sent people to
find out their
intentions. He
ordered that the visitors
be offered jewels and feathers and,
of course, human sacrifices.

   Although disgusted by this offering, the
Spaniards settled down some distance from the

coast. Moctezuma then changed his mind and mounted an offensive against them, dispatching his best sorcerers to bewitch the intruders.

The Spaniards Were Immovable, and Moctezuma Continually Hesitated About What to Do

In fact, the emperor did not really know whether he should receive Cortés as a god or as his worst enemy. Should he offer sumptuous hospitality and be conciliatory, or should he try by all possible means to turn the Spaniard's plans in a different direction? Perhaps he was convinced from the start that his end was unavoidable—this theory would explain his constant changes of mind, from resignation to indignation. This conviction may also have incited him to abdicate his powers, even before the ultimate confrontation with the Spanish.

For the present the Spanish, insensitive to native magic because their flesh was "hard," that is, impenetrable by evil spells, left the coastal region and marched on Tenochtitlán. They had decided to see things through to the end.

"Doña Marina had been a great lady and a cacique [chief] over towns and vassals since her childhood. Her father and mother were lords of a town called Paynala, which had other towns subject to it."
Bernal Díaz del Castillo,
The Conquest of New Spain,
16th century

Here Marina, Cortés' mistress and interpreter, is shown standing beside him as he receives gifts (above).

Having reached the highlands, they entered
a region dominated by Tlaxcala—the Triple
Alliance's old enemy—and at first came up
against populations determined to crush
those they believed to be Moctezuma's
allies. But soon, struck by the
Spaniards' firepower and
tenacity of purpose, the
Tlaxcalans decided to support
the foreigners against the Triple Alliance.
Cortés quickly formalized a union with those
who had stood up to the Aztecs.

The Spaniards Were Received with Open Arms by the Aztecs' Enemies

Continuing their march, they halted at Cholula,
which was then an ally of the Triple Alliance.
The terrified natives witnessed the massacre of
the local nobility, who were suspected of
preparing an ambush. The Spaniards then
reached Chalco, where they received splendid
presents; the Chalca even offered their
support. At Coyoacán, at the gates of Mexico,
the Tepanec nation celebrated Cortés and
took the opportunity to offer its allegiance,
too. The Chalca, Tepanecs, Tlaxcalans—
all thirsting for revenge, all opened
breaches in the Triple Alliance's system.

On 8 November 1519 Cortés met the emperor Moctezuma at the entrance of Tenochtitlán: "When we met I dismounted and stepped forward to embrace him, but the two lords who were with him stopped me with their hands so that I should not touch him.... When at last I came to speak with Moctezuma himself, I took off a necklace of pearls and cut glass that I was wearing and placed it around his neck.... A servant of his came with two necklaces, wrapped in a cloth, made from red snails' shells, which they hold in great esteem; and from each necklace hung eight shrimps of refined gold almost a span in length. When they had been brought he turned to me and placed them about my neck, and then continued up the street...until we reached a very large and beautiful house which had been very well prepared to accommodate us."

Hernán Cortés
Letters from Mexico
1519–26

Left: A 19th-century version of the meeting. Opposite: Cortés meeting the Tlaxcalans.

Cortés missed none of the signs that indicated the Aztecs' real weaknesses: the inferiority of their weapons, Moctezuma's hesitation, and the discontent of the subject peoples.

It was probably at this point that he perceived the possibility of forming an Indian confederation in his pay against the Triple Alliance. Any doubts that he might have had left him. Having founded the country's first Spanish town at Veracruz, he was given by the elected municipal council (in reality, his own army) all necessary administrative, judiciary, and military powers for conquest and colonization, subject to Crown approval. His next moves were to scuttle his ships, removing any temptation his men might have

"As the conversation went on...we who were his friends advised him ...not to leave a single ship in port, but to destroy them all immediately, in order to leave no cause of trouble behind. For when we had marched inland others of our people might rebel like the last."
Bernal Díaz del Castillo, *The Conquest of New Spain,* 16th century

had to flee or seek new adventures, and to settle in enemy territory.

Cortés Was Eager to Meet the Master of the Aztec World and Discover the Extent of His Wealth and the Reality of His Powers

At the same moment, Moctezuma, always prone to paralyzing indecision, called together the rulers of Texcoco and Tacuba to organize the most sumptuous of receptions. All the great dignitaries and princes were invited to be present as the Spaniards arrived. Cortés and his party were followed by native bearers bent double under the weight of the presents accumulated along the way.

Cortés orders the ships to be destroyed (below).

Moctezuma, the "image of Huitzilopochtli," borne on his precious palanquin by lords, surrounded by his court and a multitude of slaves carrying offerings for the gods, went to meet Cortés.

The two processions came face to face. The sovereign placed a necklace of gold and precious stones around the Spaniard's neck and gave him a splendid flower made of feathers. Then they entered a nearby temple, where they received the homage of the rulers of Texcoco and Tacuba. The great dignitaries and lords came to worship Cortés, just as they did the god Huitzilopochtli. Moctezuma evoked the power that he derived from his "father," the god Quetzalcoatl, whom he was ready to renounce; Cortés replied that he came in the name of a powerful lord, who reigned over a

Illustrations of Cortés at Moctezuma's court, painted in 1698.

"Moctezuma came to greet us and with him some two hundred lords, all barefoot and dressed in a different costume, but also very rich in their way and more so than the others."
Hernán Cortés
Letters from Mexico
1519–26

great part of the globe, and of the one true God. From this meeting one can see that the Aztecs and the Spaniards were in different worlds.

Whether by Calculation or Resignation, Moctezuma Submitted to His New Masters and Was Betrayed

The procession set off to Tenochtitlán, where it was greeted by the priests, amid the sound of trumpets and conch shells. Cortés and his people were lodged in the Palace of Axayácatl.

Moctezuma and the other lords were immediately detained by the Spaniards and placed under guard.

Since the Aztecs still had superior forces, some Spaniards wanted to strike a great blow immediately. So, after receiving reinforcements, they asked to be

"Then he raised his clothes and showed me his body, saying, as he grasped his arms and trunk with his hands, 'See that I am of flesh and blood like you....' When he had gone we were well provided with chickens, bread, fruit, and other requisites.... In this manner I spent six days...."

Hernán Cortés
Letters from Mexico
1519–26

present at the ritual dances in celebration of the feast of Huitzilopochtli. This occasion provided them with an ideal opportunity to assemble and then massacre the most eminent members of the Aztec nobility. They are said to have killed almost ten thousand Aztecs. Moctezuma died, mortally wounded by one of his own people (unless he was executed by the Spaniards—there is still some doubt). Cacamatzin, ruler of Texcoco, and the governor of Tlatelolco were strangled.

The *Noche Triste*: Determined to Confront the Spaniards, the Aztecs Fought Back

The surviving Aztec aristocrats did not surrender and were determined to finish off the invaders. After the brief reign of Cuitláhuac, the young nephew of Moctezuma, Cuauhtémoc, who would be the last Aztec emperor, took over. The Aztecs surrounded the palaces where the Spaniards were living, with the firm intention of exterminating them. Once more, however, the Spaniards managed to save their skins.

On 30 June 1520, taking advantage of a moonless night and torrential rain, the Spaniards fled. Although they suffered extremely heavy losses, they reached the mainland. The Aztecs harried them, and thought themselves rid of these intruders forever. It is said that Cortés wept at dawn when he realized the scale of the disaster of what was to be called the *Noche Triste* (Sad Night). But he was not to give up Tenochtitlán.

Through Otumba, where he killed the head of the Aztec army with his own hand, he opened up the route to Tlaxcala. There he prepared a tremendous offensive against the Aztec capital, exploiting the dissensions that split the indigenous world. Cuauhtémoc failed to rally all the domains against the Spaniards. The Texcocans, the Chalca, and the Tepanecs—all those which Tenochtitlán had previously subjugated or humiliated—took the side of the Spaniards.

At Texcoco, on the lake's eastern shore, one of Nezahualpilli's sons, Ixtlilxóchitl, put all his energy into supporting Cortés. The ruin of the Triple Alliance

came about through the tensions between the domains as much as through a tragic miscalculation: The enemies of Tenochtitlán, especially the Tlaxcalans, believed that the Spaniards were going to help them eliminate the Aztecs. They never suspected they were to be the next victims of a power whose resources and ambition they badly underestimated.

The Nightmare Siege of Tenochtitlán Remains Etched in Aztec Memory

Cortés besieged the city for three whole months. His troops expanded by several

After the death of Moctezuma, while a prisoner of the Spaniards, his brother Cuitláhuac and nephew Cuauhtémoc became the leaders of the Aztecs. Cortés was besieged and resolved to leave the city. On a rainy night, the *Noche Triste,* the Spaniards succeeded in reaching one of the highways linking Tenochtitlán to the shore. But the Aztecs, once alerted, attacked: More than half the Spaniards and almost all their native auxiliaries were killed or taken prisoner.

thousand Indians, he was quick to construct a flotilla of brigantines to secure control of the lake. The Spaniards cut off Tenochtitlán's fresh water and food supplies, and attacked relentlessly. An epidemic of European disease, to which the Indians had no resistance, also took a toll, and finally, despite the Aztecs' ferocious

Cortés prepared his revenge for the *Noche Triste* by reconstituting his artillery and cavalry, and especially by building a small fleet of thirteen brigantines, thus overcoming his main military weakness, his inability to move around on water.

resistance, the city fell on 13 August 1521. According to the 17th-century chronicler Alva Ixtlilxóchitl, "Almost all the Aztec nobility died, the only survivors being a few lords and gentlemen, mostly children or extremely young people." Cuauhtémoc was taken prisoner and kept alive for a while, but then hanged on the pretext of his involvement in a plot. In all, 240,000 people are said to have died in Tenochtitlán.

The Aztec empire had collapsed. Cortés continued the conquest, and a year later, in 1522, he became governor and captain-general of New Spain.

The conquistador replaced the Triple Alliance with the distant authority of an unknown emperor who reigned beyond the ocean over Spain: Charles V. There were no longer any shifting coalitions, regularly questioning each other's supremacy. The Spaniards' weapons, tactics, and energy were undoubtedly very important factors, but one should not overlook the fact that the conquistadors' victory was won by a coalition of numerous states and peoples.

A fter the *Noche Triste* and Cortés' desperate flight from Tenochtitlán, an Aztec army tried, at Otumba (below), to cut short the retreat of Cortés and his Spaniards. After a tough battle the Spaniards, who suffered dramatic losses, finally emerged victorious and returned to Tlaxcala to recover their strength. There they dressed their wounds and prepared for the decisive assault on Tenochtitlán.

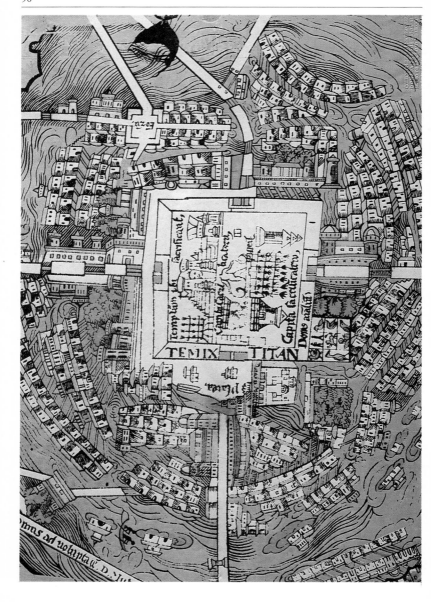

TEMIX TITAN

Those who had been the masters were not all resigned to defeat. Part of the Mexica and Texcocan aristocracy cherished the hope that the invaders would eventually leave. The "anti-Spanish party" stubbornly believed in the restoration of the old order. Cortés set out to shatter these illusions.

CHAPTER V

FROM RESISTANCE TO COLLABORATION

Sixteenth-century plan of the Aztec city of Tenochtitlán. Below: Torture by savage dogs.

Cortés did not just impose submission to the Spanish Crown; he also demanded that the Indians convert to Christianity. He ordered an end to human sacrifices everywhere and installed images of the new divinities in the native sanctuaries: the Virgin, Christ, the saints. The Indians were astounded by the violence and passion with which the conquistadors broke the statues of their gods, whom they gave the defamatory name of idols. Cortés' conduct was inspired as much by gold and a love of power as by a desire to propagate the Christian faith—because this faith both justified his enterprise and, in the spirit of the times, gave it a goal and a meaning.

From 1525 on, with the arrival of a small but determined contingent of Franciscans, the Aztec clergy was brutally forced to leave its sanctuaries and practice its rites in secret. The Spaniards carried out raids against the temples, assassinated pagan priests, set fire to the pyramids, smashed the statues, and burned codices covered in pictographs. Iconoclastic violence replaced that of the sacrifices.

Idolatry—Defined as Everything That Opposes Christianity—Became the Monster to Be Overthrown. Recalcitrant Indians Were Seen as Idolaters Inspired by the Devil

The European monks succeeded in winning over part of the elite. Their success was indeed spectacular, as is shown by the hundreds of thousands of baptisms that the chroniclers of the time imperturbably recorded.

It is true that in these chaotic times, the years 1530–40, the monks introduced some semblance of order: Around their churches and monasteries, under their often discretionary authority, life could reorganize itself. New rituals replaced the banned celebrations, new powers were substituted for those overthrown by the conquistadors.

The monks quickly became a force to be reckoned with, a force that could counterbalance the excesses of the Spanish soldiers and their native collaborators.

"The idols are made of dough from all the seeds and vegetables which they eat, ground and mixed together, and bound with the blood of human hearts which those priests tear out while still beating...after they are made they offer them more hearts."
Hernán Cortés
Letters from Mexico
1519–26

At San Juan de Ulúa, near Veracruz, faced with the repeated refusal of the cacique to recant his beliefs, Cortés seized him, entered the temple, to the great alarm of the pagan priests and the people, and cast down the idols. The next day Father Bartolomeo de Olmedo, a monk of the Order of Mercy, celebrated the holy sacrament.

This state of affairs was even more of a blow for the "idolaters" who saw their influence being undermined and their legitimacy called into question.

The Arrival of Christianity Shook the Native Societies to Their Very Foundations

The "anti-Spanish party" rejected not only the new regime but also the new religious order, or rather the revolution brought about by Christianity, because its creed imposed a break with the past in condemning a great many of the principles by which the nobility had lived.

In the various sermons of the gospel-preachers, the ancestors of the Aztecs, the prestigious Toltecs, became monstrous idolaters condemned to burn for all eternity in the flames of hell. Christianity closed the schools where the nobility had always learned the ancient knowledge; it forbade human sacrifice, the consumption of the victims' flesh (that is, ritual cannibalism), and polygamy. Finally, it proscribed the taking of hallucinogenic plants. All these practices and privileges had always distinguished those in power from the common people and maintained their legitimacy.

By Imposing a Uniform System of Marriage, the Church Destroyed the Traditional Practice of Alliances Throughout the Empire

Conversion, in particular, posed a threat to family cohesion—not only through the forced transition to monogamy, which threw thousands of secondary wives into the street with their children (who became bastards without a name or a future), but also because

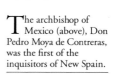

The archbishop of Mexico (above), Don Pedro Moya de Contreras, was the first of the inquisitors of New Spain.

Former Aztec practices (left).

A Dominican friar preaches to the Aztecs (opposite).

the preachers did not hesitate to seize the children of the nobility to Christianize them and use them against their recalcitrant parents. The monks were well aware of the adults' resistance, so they chose to educate the young nobles in schools where they were taught the catechism, reading, and writing. The children, thus converted, became their agents and spies.

Something else that scandalized the Aztec aristocracy was that the Christian religion claimed that all people were equal before God and entrusted the powerful with the spiritual and general well-being of the humble. This attitude was truly unacceptable for a nobility that believed an impassable physical and spiritual barrier separated it from the rest of humanity.

The conversion of the Indians to Christianity was organized with brutal efficiency. Opposite: Spanish soldiers destroy Aztec idols. Above: Baptism of the lords of Tlaxcala. Below: The first church in Texcoco.

Convinced that Christianity Meant the Overthrow of Their System of Values, the "Idolaters" Tried to Resist the Spanish Invader

But the attempts at conspiracy and at boycotting Spanish orders failed through lack of organization. Those who opposed Christianity were rapidly forced to go underground or hand over their weapons. In any case, how could one live a clandestine life when power had always gone hand in hand with spectacular display?

The opposition disappeared little by little, through summary execution, accident, or disease. One of the spokesmen in Texcoco was burned at the stake in 1539 for saying too loudly what many people were thinking at the time.

Other nobles, whether resigned to their fate, powerless, opportunistic, or sincere, chose to collaborate. In this way they reckoned they might hold on to their most important powers, because they knew they possessed a precious trump card: their knowledge of people and terrain. Certainly the conquistadors had to rely on the native nobles taking over some roles if they wanted to extend their control over this immense territory, draw up an inventory of its resources, and exploit them to their advantage.

The Changing Role of the Nobility

Besides Nahuatl, over a hundred languages were spoken in New Spain. For this reason, the monks set out to Christianize the ruling class in the hope that the rest of the population would follow its lead. Members of the nobility did indeed prove to be the best allies of the preachers in their missionary aims.

In the first years collaboration with the victors paid off. The lords of Tlaxcala began this policy by being baptized, thus enabling them to retain relative autonomy until the end of the century. At Texcoco members of the ruling family also played the Spanish card; they made a decisive contribution in crushing the Mexica and helped the start of Franciscan evangelization.

The ambitions of yesteryear were henceforth reduced to very little: After having played the role of indispensable intermediaries between the invaders and the rest of the population, the great families gradually had to content themselves with the role of rich people of standing, with only local influence. As for Texcoco itself, it was eclipsed by the capital of New Spain, chosen by Cortés, Mexico City.

The Beginnings of Intermarriage

The daughters of the native aristocracy frequently became the conquerors' concubines and sometimes even legitimate wives.

Moctezuma's daughter, Tecuichpotzin, is an excellent example of this. The wife of the

Father Bartolomeo de Olmedo was entrusted by Cortés with baptizing the Aztecs. An intelligent man and an excellent theologian, he often intervened to moderate the conquistador's ardor and brutality.

last two Aztec monarchs, Cuitláhuac and Cuauhtémoc, in rapid succession, she was baptized after the conquest and given the name Isabella. Widowed by Cuauhtémoc at the age of sixteen, she still embodied a certain Aztec legitimacy, and constituted a figure of some importance

R aising the cross in an Aztec town.

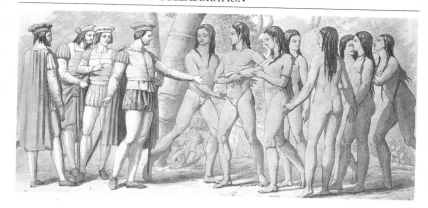

on the new political chessboard. Cortés awarded her the revenues of the city of Tacuba in perpetuity, and then had her marry the conquistador Alonso de Grado. This Indian lady soon became a model of Hispanization and Christian piety. After Grado's death she lived for a while in Cortés' "harem," bore him a daughter, then remarried Spaniards on two occasions. Her last husband actively busied himself with increasing their fortune and pleading for her rights as Moctezuma II's heiress. She died in 1550, a very wealthy woman, after she had drawn up her will.

Her daughter Leonor was to marry the discoverer of the silver mines of Zacatecas, and some of her descendants would settle in Spain, where they took the titles of the Count of Miravalle, Duke of Abrantés, and Duke of Linares.

Other families had less glittering but probably more typical destinies. For example, the mother and grandmother of Alva Ixtlilxóchitl, direct heirs of the rulers of Texcoco, married Spaniards who also undertook to defend their interests.

The marriages between native princesses and conquistadors and their offspring undeniably facilitated the transition between the two worlds.

The Ruling Class Was Renewed, and Some People Took Advantage of the Opportunity to Denounce the Old Aristocracy

Minor provincial nobles and plebeians took advantage of the favor of the conquistadors and the Church to get involved in the circles of leadership. So they swelled the ranks of the collaborators, and the traditional nobility was reduced to sharing the title of cacique—as well as the role of governor given to them by the Spanish regime—with these "upstarts." Elected or nominated governors, these natives found themselves at the head of local populations grouped into communities, the *pueblos de indios*, which after 1530 were endowed with

"The old cacique of Tlaxcala, Xicotenga, made this remark to Cortés: 'To prove still more clearly how much we love you and wish to please you in all things, we want to give you our daughters for wives to bear you children.'"

Bernal Díaz del Castillo,
The Conquest of New Spain,
16th century

Lám. 1.

CORDILLERA
DE LOS
PUEBLOS,
QUE
ANTES DE LA CONQUISTA
PAGABAN TRIBUTO
A EL EMPERADOR
MUCTEZUMA,
Y
EN QUE ESPECIE,
Y
CANTIDAD.

The Spaniards had left Tabasco with twenty native women given to them by those they had conquered (opposite above). One of them, Malinche, a young Aztec baptized Marina by the Spanish, became Cortés' mistress as well as his interpreter (opposite below).

institutions transferred from Spain.

However, the Spanish Crown was not always in favor of founding new elites. Toward the middle of the 16th century it even tried to reinstall the heirs of the former lords everywhere it seemed possible to do so, because it believed that the transference of power was compatible with respect for native hierarchies, providing that Spain's sovereignty was recognized.

From the very beginning the Crown sought to create and safeguard an "Indian" identity, taking care to keep separate the indigenous and Spanish communities—or the two "republics," to use the term of the period; the control of the native population had to remain in the hands of the native nobility.

In this way they preserved the role of obligatory intermediary that was adopted by the legitimate or upstart caciques. It also meant that the term "Indian" was established, henceforth designating all the natives, whatever their rank or their ethnic origin.

The Fall of Mexico in No Way Signaled the End of Military Campaigns for the Aztecs, Who Found Employment in the Service of the Crown

In the 1520s the pacifying of the center of the country and the conquest of Guatemala and Honduras were carried out with the support of the valley's nobility and their troops. These same forces were to push back the attacks of the Chichimec Indians and guarantee access to northern Mexico's silver mines.

From 1541 to 1542 several tens of thousands of Mexica, Tlaxcalans, and Otomís crushed the rebellion *ſuys pinello nahuatlan* of Mixton, in the northwest part of the country, some four hundred miles from Mexico City. The bravest fighters among the Indians won military ranks there, together with coats of arms and titles, while throughout the 16th century their troops settled locally, in exchange for a few privileges.

Spanish colonization reversed the old pattern: After this time it was to be "civilized" Indians from the center of the country who moved northward to impose their sedentary ways on the nomads. Nothing could stop the retreat of the wild Indians, which continued its bloody progress until the 19th century.

From the 1540s on the new or traditional native ruling class promptly adapted to the world taking shape before its eyes. Not only did these people quickly become familiar with handling weapons and horses, but they learned bookkeeping, branched out into stockrearing or business, bought the goods being exported by Spain to its young colony, drank wine, and wore silks. They even acquired a sufficient mastery of Spanish legislation to make it work in their favor and defend their rights. This world of judges, governors, merchants, and interpreters carved itself a place in colonial society, in the shadow of the conquerors but above the masses.

The association of traditional pictographs with commentaries in Spanish shows how the two cultures came together at the time of the conquest: This account book (left) shows the officials involved and lists the types of services and objects supplied. Account books in codex form, like this one, were used very early on to record the economic, commercial, and financial transformations introduced by the invaders.

Coat of arms of Spain (below) in the reign of Philip II (1556–98).

The Church's Education and the Indians' Incredible Ability to Assimilate Bore Unexpected and Remarkable Fruit

Ironically, the meeting of cultures allowed a late flourishing in Mexico of the European renaissance. This renaissance found expression in the works of the native painters and sculptors who took part in building the churches, monasteries, and chapels that now covered New Spain. Besides these masters of stone and brush, who were in keeping with the best pre-Hispanic tradition, there were also musicians and singers who proliferated in most settlements, learning the instruments of medieval Europe and, in some cases, tackling composition with a vigor that staggered the Spaniards.

But the most profound revolution was undoubtedly tied to the introduction of the European alphabet and, consequently, to the learning of writing. These Indians, whose culture had for centuries been based on pictographs and an oral tradition, learned to read and write under the monks' guidance.

Higher education was even provided for the most gifted at the college of Santa Cruz at Tlatelolco. They learned the language of Cicero, read the Latin classics, and translated great European texts into Nahuatl. Some even familiarized themselves with typography and printing. Many became indispensable witnesses for the Franciscan and Dominican monks when they made their great ethnographic investigations into the pre-conquest societies. Others were to contribute to the knowledge of history.

The adoption of writing did not mean abandoning illustrated codices. Not only were the historians Chimalpahin, Ixtlilxóchitl, and Tezozómoc still able to understand them, but well-read Indians learned to combine the pictographic tradition with European writing. They succeeded in making maximum use of

The indigenous painter Juan Gerson produced frescoes of the apocalypse of Tecamachalco. Like his contemporaries, he mixed indigenous and European elements in his compositions. The Indian painters succeeded in expressing colonial reality while meeting Spanish demands and remaining faithful to their art. It is probable that the systematic subjugation of the native elements to western iconographic conventions diverted them from their original meaning and usage, but out of this confrontation arose a unique artistic expression.

these two modes of expression with an inventiveness and intelligence that display the astonishing fruitfulness of this period and of these well-to-do circles. But this renaissance was to be smothered by the colonial machine.

On the Other Hand, Throughout the 16th Century, the Indian Masses Were Devastated by the Shock of Conquest: Epidemics, Ruthless Exploitation, and Shattered Values

Chaos took numerous forms. The ancestral guidelines that marked the differences between classes and origins foundered. The many signs of status disappeared— ostentatious clothing, participation in solemn celebrations, and food privileges, which had reserved cacao, hallucinogens, and the divine flesh of sacrificial victims for the nobles.

The power vacuum was also formidable: In 1521 the nobles and leaders tragically proved themselves powerless to oppose the foreigners. Even more serious was the death of the gods. From the end of the 1520s on, amid the general confusion and under pressure from the preachers, the sacrifices and cults that had always marked the cycles of time and ensured the working of the cosmos were interrupted, or definitively abandoned. All the institutional frameworks that upheld the old societies were called into question or broken, with nothing to replace them apart from the Christianity propagated by the Franciscans in a few cities.

An illustration from a codex with native pictographs and Spanish text, produced in 1554 under the instructions of a Spanish missionary. The missionaries found pictures to be a handy means—especially at first—of overcoming their ignorance of the Indian languages.

Until the 1540s there was arbitrary rule. The conquistadors plundered, reduced the Indians to slavery, branded them with hot irons, and worked them to exhaustion; the

extortions of the caciques often rivaled those of the Spaniards. Not content with eliminating the former priests and part of the nobility, the Spaniards reserved the priesthood for themselves and had a monopoly on the sacred and hence on the meaning of existence.

However, it was especially by using a different language—it is extremely doubtful whether most Indians could catch its exact meaning—that Christianity and the Church destroyed not only the rules of the way of life, but the way of life itself. There was total disarray, as can be seen in this testimony from one of the native Indians: "The great freedom we now enjoy is pernicious because we are no longer forced to fear or respect anyone."

On Top of Everything, Epidemics

The scourge harvested its regular tribute of human lives. We do not know the precise nature of the illnesses that killed the Indians, commoners and nobles alike. Types of typhus and smallpox spread from the time of the siege of Tenochtitlán. Epidemics broke out in the whole country and raged almost continuously, with marked outbreaks in 1545–8, 1581–6, and 1629–31.

The lack of successful treatments, the moral and cultural distress, the human exhaustion, and the absence of acquired immunity all explain the enormous mortality rate. Scared by the drop in population, the Spaniards tried to understand the cause of this phenomenon that was depriving them of a precious labor force and a large amount of tribute. Seized with panic, the Indians attributed these catastrophes to the destruction of their way of life, the Spaniards' cruelty, and the abandonment of the old gods. Most often they were simply dazed by their misfortune.

In the face of death's repeated assaults and the collapse of traditional institutions, many Indians turned to alcohol, the pre-Hispanic prohibitions having been swept aside. Infanticides and suicides multiplied, an expression of the unbearable tragedy that these populations were experiencing.

All the medical knowledge of the Aztec doctors was helpless against the implacable plague of epidemics brought by the Spaniards (right). The illnesses were attributed to supernatural causes, to the will of gods, or the magic of sorcerers. The doctor *(ticitl)* resorted to divination, counter-magic, or the laying-on of hands. In other cases Aztec doctors could be more effective: They knew how to set fractures, apply plasters, carry out bleedings, and above all prepare potions with medicinal plants.

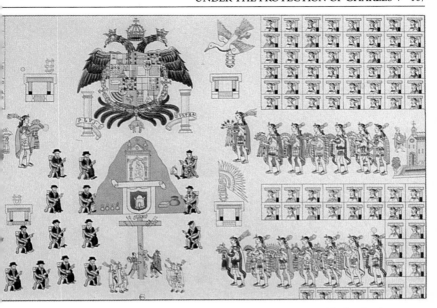

The break with former times merely began with the Spanish conquest. It would continue throughout the 16th century and into the 17th. There was no end to the death throes of a whole universe. It was left to the handful of survivors to construct another world.

Painted at the request of the viceroy, Don Luis de Velasco, between 1550 and 1564, the *Codex Lienzo de Tlaxcala* is a work measuring about 23 x 8 feet that depicts the Tlaxcalan version of the conquest in eighty-seven images. In the one above, governors, viceroys, and lords of Tlaxcala can be seen under the coat of arms of Charles V.

In the 17th century the indigenous society disintegrated, shattered by the chaos that struck colonial Mexico. Even though some members of the nobility continued proudly to assert their pre-Hispanic origins, their way of life was no longer anything but a replica, more or less faithful, of the Spanish model.

CHAPTER VI
THE AFTERMATH OF THE CONQUEST

Toward the end of the 16th century there were already more than 25,000 people of mixed blood in Mexico. Fifty years later there were 400,000, and two centuries after that their numbers reached 1.5 million. This population grew rapidly because the Spanish immigrants were mostly male. Opposite: An 18th-century painting of a family of mixed racial origin. Left: *Carmelita*, a 19th-century sculpture.

Without really disappearing, the native nobility was increasingly submerged in an intermediate racial world in which its identity was eventually dissolved.

How to Retain One's Indigenous Identity While Adapting to the Spanish Model

This nobility now had to spare no effort in protecting the integrity of its patrimony and ensuring that the rank Spain had conceded to it was passed on, for imposters managed to infiltrate the caciques, despite lawsuits that sometimes dragged on for generations. Shaken by sordid quarrels, noble families of long standing sank into ruin, and with that the memory of ancient times became blurred.

Nevertheless, in the mid-18th century there were still nobles powerful enough to constitute an important native pressure group in Mexico and Tlaxcala.

This group was closely tied to the Church and very proud of its blood and its origins; it continued to combine fortune, power, and culture. Its spokespeople did not hesitate to visit Spain to plead the cause of the Mexican caciques and, if necessary, to demand loudly that the Indian population should be given the benefits of an education that would bring it out of the "darkness of ignorance," "because, when deprived of education, the natives' only rationale is what nature instills in them."

This nobility learned the 16th-century missionaries' lessons

The Spanish government first watched the conquistadors from afar, leaving them more or less free to do as they chose. But then it determined that they should not enjoy the powers they were claiming for very long. In November 1529 the sovereign chose one of his civil servants, a loyal, prudent, and hardworking lord, to be his representative in Mexico with very extensive powers. Installed in 1535, Antonio de Mendoza was the first—and also one of the most remarkable—of the sixty-two viceroys who successively governed Mexico for almost three centuries.

Three great administrators, Antonio de Mendoza (1535–49), Luis de Velasco (1550–64), and Martín Enríquez (1568–80), gave Mexico a period of calm throughout the 16th century that enabled the conquest to continue and the country's economy to take a new course that was favorable to Spanish interests. The viceroy's palaces (right) dominated the towns and impressed the native lords (left).

112

FORMA Y LEVANTADO DE LA
Por la correspondencia d̃ los numéres s̃e hallan en est̃

N.º 1. Conuentos de S. Fran.co   4. q̃ son s.n Fran.co S. Tiago S. Diego S.ta Maria Lo Redonda   N.º 7. Monxas
N.º 2. DE S.t Augustin   4. S.n Augustin S. Pablo S. Anastasia, S. Cruz   N.º 8. Hospitales
N.º 3. De S. Domingo   2. q̃ son S. Domingo y Porta Cæli   N.º 9. Paroquias
N.º 4. Padres de La Comp.a   Casa professa los estudios S. Hilefons S. Anna noueccina   N.º 10. Colegios
N.º 5. Mercenarios   2. Nuestra S.ra La merced y Ntra. S.ra de Belem
N.º 6. Ntra S.ra DEL Carmen   y N.ra Senora de Montserrate
                              Suma 18.   Suma

A. Palacio Re.l
B. Cathedral.
C. Casa de Cabildo.
D. Casa Arpl.
F. Uniuersidad.
G. Alameda.
Las Demas casas estan Señaladas por
su Demostracion como as distinto partes
por la Plana.

Jo: gen.l de trasmonte il 1628.

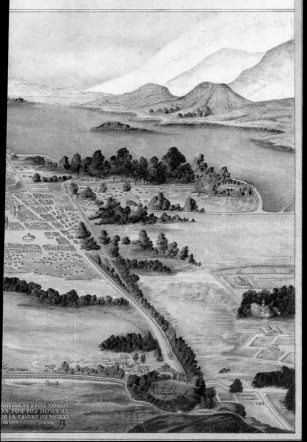

At the end of the 18th century and the beginning of the 19th, the capital of New Spain, with its 137,000 inhabitants, was the most populous city in the New World. It boasted a cathedral, baronial halls, buildings to house new industries (tobacco factories), and new institutions like the College of Mines and the Academy of Fine Arts of San Carlos. The urbanization ordered by the viceroy Antonio María de Bucareli y Ursúa and his successors made the city cleaner and more beautiful. The viceroys paved the streets, laid sidewalks, and drained sewage and dirty water. A public utility provided street lighting, as in the time of Moctezuma.

From Pyramid to Cathedral

Along the Zócalo (city square) in Mexico City, the largest cathedral in Mexico displays its beautiful, mostly baroque facade of gray stone between two squat neoclassical towers. Begun in 1573, after the municipal council presented a request to Philip II, king of Spain, begging him to grant permission to erect a new cathedral worthy of the opulence of the New World, it was not until 1813 that it was completely finished. This cathedral replaced the very modest church built just after the conquest with materials taken from the pyramid of Huitzilopochtli, on a site located a little to the northwest of the present cathedral. The baroque part of the facade has three doors flanked by columns and surmounted by niches with carved ornamentation. All the differences of style in the cathedral bear witness to the fact that its construction was the work of several generations of architects.

so well, along with the prejudices of the period, that it picked up the torch of Christianity, helped by those of its members who belonged to the Catholic clergy.

In the face of the splintering of the great pre-conquest ethnic and political groups, the collapse of memories, and the epidemics, the Indians withdrew at the end of the 16th century to a community space around those

In 1531, north of the capital city, the Virgin supposedly appeared to a man called Juan Diego. Since then many devoted people have visited the sanctuary of Our Lady of Guadalupe at the site.

who administered the village. From the mid-17th century one of the aims of these minor dignitaries was to legitimize their power by forging themselves an identity and a place in colonial society. With this objective in mind they drew up and passed on title deeds that placed on record the history of the *pueblo,* the villagers.

Christianity Appeared as a Crucial Stage in the *Pueblo*'s History

Far from being the exclusive prerogative of the nobles, alphabetic writing also helped people in the Mexican

The Indians continued to live in their traditional homes, cooking the food that they had always eaten. But some things changed: There is a painting of the Virgin on the wall, and the facade of the local church appears through the door.

countryside to set down community memories. In these title deeds, the Christianization of the Indians, which had happened a century earlier, was no longer interpreted as a brutal coercion. The Church was now presented as the community's new axis, because it was the place where rituals occurred that punctuated existence (baptisms, marriages, and

Opposite: *The Different Races Established Since the Spanish Conquest,* a 16th-century painting.

funerals). The choice of patron saint was seen, with the passing years, as a native initiative, and by the 17th century legends described how the saint revealed his desire to take the *pueblo* under his protection.

The *Pueblo* Authorities Struggled Desperately Against Those Who Tried to Reduce Their Rights and Interfere With Their Lives

It was essentially the great Spanish landlords, the *hacendados,* and the parish priests who accorded the *pueblo*'s prerogatives the least recognition. The 17th and 18th centuries were filled with conflicts and lawsuits between Indians and *hacendados.* The native population having been depleted by epidemics, at first there were great swaths of land open to Spanish settlement. But when, during the 18th century, the Indian population began growing again, and there was no longer enough land, disputes multiplied. After the second half of the 18th century, tensions increased and violent revolts broke out.

Clashes with the priests were of a different kind, though they could be equally violent: In Indian eyes, it was a question of defending the status quo that allowed them to organize the community's religious life in their own way. Thus, whatever the adversary, it was within the framework of the *pueblo* that the natives applied themselves to preserving their patrimony of rights and beliefs, a colonial patrimony that in fact was an amalgamation of indigenous and European elements.

While the Dignitaries Forged a New Community Identity, the Masses Survived in a Colonial Society

For the people, there seemed to have been no major changes in living and working, despite a century of Spanish domination. The soil, the house, and the maize fields retained their ancient force that people had been trying to placate from time immemorial.

Yet by the first half of the 17th century, even before the end of the great epidemics, the survivors contrived

In the eyes of the Spanish colonists, the Indians represented first and foremost a work force, indeed beasts of burden (below). Even before the end of the 16th century, Mexico's economic and social evolution began to transform the organization of native labor, with the rise and development of the great Spanish domains, the haciendas, which grew up outside the towns alongside the *pueblos.* Opposite: Haciendas and settlement of a typical Mexican town, as depicted in a 17th-century Spanish print.

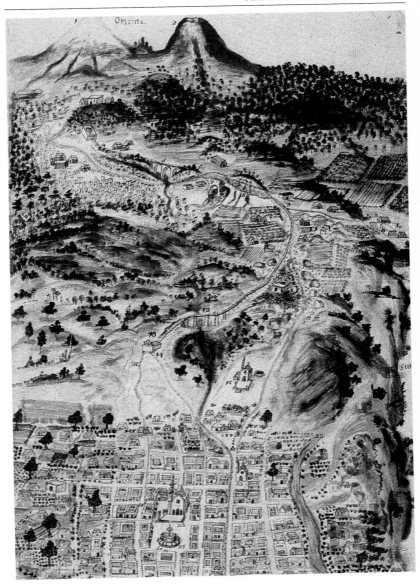

At Cuautitlán the crowds of Indians came from many miles around, on foot or donkey, to bring their vows and prayers and offer their gifts and fireworks, begging for help. The Virgin of Guadalupe remained the most venerated throughout Mexico. The processions (left) were also the occasion for parading through the town with baroque statues, which were often in painted wood and terrifyingly realistic, displaying a clear predilection for depicting bloody wounds and stigmata.

to restore some meaning and balance to their existence by blending the cult of traditional powers—fire, water, the "mountain inhabitants," or winds—with that of the saints who henceforth protected their village and home.

Little by little the Indians invented practices, beliefs, and gestures of which there are still traces in the indigenous cultures today. The 17th century saw the flowering of a unique Christianity which allowed the Indians to express what remained of their original identity through an abundance of family devotions, the development of brotherhoods, and the profusion of festivals. Calvary chapels, miraculous images, carnivals, processions, and pilgrimages gave the valleys of Mexico and Puebla an ever-increasing resemblance to the Mediterranean countryside. Out of these colonized and colonial cultures there arose a reinvented Christianity.

After the 17th Century the Virgin of Guadalupe Constituted a Widely Popular Cult

Contact with the people of various racial origins who moved into the countryside caused this Christianity to undergo a further evolution in the 18th century. There now took shape a common culture that mixed all kinds of beliefs and practices, foreshadowing the popular cultures of modern Mexico, into which the indigenous heritage gradually dissolved.

Yet it was in the towns that true change occurred, especially in the capital of New Spain. Here, starting in the 16th century, the indigenous people became familiar with the Spanish tongue and also underwent the experience of all kinds of biological, social, and cultural interbreeding.

They learned to move between two worlds, that of the Spanish masters in whose service they obtained posts, and that of a community where the constraints sometimes became unbearable.

Assimilation and Anonymity

Many of them were bilingual and knew how to use their origins to advantage or to benefit from assimilation and anonymity. By the 17th century neither their clothing nor their haircuts seemed to distinguish them from the Spanish population any longer.

Like a magnet the city attracted the

In each parish, the priest generally had three sacramental registers: one for the whites, another for the Indians, and the third for those of mixed blood. More-or-less official classifications had been established that distinguished up to sixteen categories of mixed blood depending on the respective proportions of European, Indian, or black blood. Legally superior to people of mixed blood, in actuality the Indians often held a lower social position. Intermarriage (left) confused the issue.

Indians from the villages, either because they were over-exploited or because they had resolved to break their community ties. This was a fascination that dated back a long time—one recalls the nomads who prowled around the Toltec cities centuries before in order to glean some fragments of civilization.

The West Set Its Traps: The Hope of Easy Gains and Pleasures, the Lure of Alcohol, the Illusion of Escaping One's Origins

In cities the Indians very soon assimilated the negative aspects of "culture" brought by the Spaniards. The most spectacular expression was drunkenness or, rather, alcoholism, which struck a great part of the indigenous population.

The bars, or *pulquerías,* were the setting for sordid scenes: Due to the influence of alcohol, money was squandered, bloody brawls broke out, and prostitution was carried on. In 1784 the capital had 150,000 inhabitants and more than six hundred *pulquerías,* each of which could easily contain a hundred customers, inside and out. It is also true to say that it was in the *pulquerías,* away from the parish and community, that a new society developed, a demimonde of people of mixed racial heritage.

On the other hand, the taverns were also places for relaxing. These *pulquerías* were alternatives to a rigid society that sought to assign everyone a fixed place depending on their race and wealth, and in many ways were the crucible from which the popular

In the 17th century and even at the beginning of the 18th the preparation of the alcoholic drink pulque was still accompanied by ritual practices and burnt offerings, and the drinking sessions that attended the brotherhood festivals, funerals, and Christian solemnities, even in the great cities, all echoed the collective ceremonies before the conquest. But by the late 18th and 19th centuries the *pulquerías* showed the influence of the conquerors (opposite above).

By 1750 no less than ten thousand Indians had migrated to the towns, employed ever since as porters, bearers, water sellers, tortilla vendors, and servants (opposite below and left).

culture of modern Mexico was to arise.

By the second half of the 16th century, a reduced, uprooted, and mobile population was discovering in the silver mines the pressures of salaried work in more-or-less permanent and specialized teams.

In one generation these workers went through stages of acculturation that it took others several centuries to achieve.

Like the mines, forced labor in those prisonlike workshops known as *obrajes* wore people out in body and soul by tearing them away from their family circle and delivering them to an unfamiliar, frenzied, and dead-end way of life.

For other native people, however, craftsmaking, selling foodstuffs, and employment as servants offered less painful avenues that allowed them to get along in the world with at least some form of employment, however limited.

In the 19th Century the Native Mexicans Faced the First Onslaught of the Modern World

Paradoxically it was the ideals of the Enlightenment and independence that again brought into question the Indian way of life, abruptly upsetting the balance that the indigenous communities had recovered with such difficulty. Anxious to educate (no longer to Christianize, as in the 16th century), the state intervened and imposed schoolmasters everywhere, together with the teaching of the Spanish tongue. In the same period, around 1780, it was preoccupied with economies, and set out to abolish or severely restrict the most spectacular features of native culture: religious theater, brotherhoods, processions, and festivals. The Crown was of the same mind, and was soon to revise its

A crucial institution of ancient Mexican societies, the tradition of the almost daily market lasted through the centuries. This institution conserved all its vigor and, with colonization, took on an extra meaning: The market was no longer just the place for making deals around such commodities as highly individual textiles (opposite above). It became the place for exchange and meetings, for the mixing of social classes and of races, as well. The marketplace was where everyone occupied the same ground and spoke a common language (left).

policy toward the communities: In the 19th century it abolished all legal difference between Indians and Spaniards. Should one hail the paternalism of an "enlightened" power that wanted to educate the native people and improve their material existence? Or perhaps one can more readily see in this more violence against a culture that was still reeling from one century of conquest and another of terrible hardship.

In the 20th century Mexico, out of concern for democracy and equality, confirmed these measures. It made the Indians citizens like any others and set out to break up and sell to individuals the communal lands from which the *pueblo* derived a good deal of its resources.

This was a death sentence for the indigenous communities, whose neighborhoods, distant heirs of pre-Hispanic Tenochtitlán and Tlatelolco, disappeared, absorbed by the modern city. Afterward the Indians could only stand aside to make way for the speculators and lose themselves in the mass of the population. Still more wrongs were to undermine the rural communities throughout the 19th century: The extension of the great landed property, the *hacienda*, was to turn the native peasants into agricultural workers who were enslaved for life, tied to their master's land, and subject to his despotism. Although the revolution of 1910 put an end to this new servitude, it could not slow down the irreversible destruction of the edifice that the Indians had rebuilt so laboriously under Spanish domination.

Are the Heirs of the Aztecs Today No More Than Images for Art Books, Figures in Comic Strips, or Characters in Revolutionary Epics?

Some villages, some enclaves resisted modernization longer than others, but the 20th century, with the abrupt rise of industrialization, opened up the era of massive migration to the cities and the final abandonment of a soil that had become incapable of feeding so many families. Near Mexico City the fauna

"Mexico today still carries the stamp of its Indian origin, the mark of those Aztecs whose language impregnates spoken Spanish, and who left enough traces of their intellectual and artistic capacities to make one look on the future of that country with confidence."

Jacques Soustelle
The Four Suns, 1957

and flora of a thousand years—and the ancestral landscape—were engulfed by the megalopolis. Is all we have left of the Aztecs a mute craft, a mixture of the heritage of distant pre-Hispanic times, the Spanish colony, and the 19th century?

And yet the Indians still exist. But they scarcely have the means any longer of escaping the onslaught of an industrial society that makes the mirages of the consumer age shimmer at the very doors of their shanty-towns. A thousand years after the Toltecs and Tula, five hundred years after the Mexica and Tenochtitlán, is there room in today's world for the Aztecs?

Tampico, today one of Mexico's leading ports, lies about six miles up the Pánuco River on the Gulf of Mexico. In 1836 (below) it was already an important town, though low-lying and subject to flooding.

Overleaf: An 18th-century depiction of Mexican Indians.

Tunas

DOCUMENTS

The Origins of the World and Its Inhabitants

In the beginning darkness ruled. The gods assembled before a light. The humblest of them fell into it: He became the sun. Thus began Aztec cosmogony.

The Five Suns

The Aztec myth of the five suns explained the inevitability of human destiny.

Here is the oral account of what is known of how the earth was founded long ago.

One by one, here are its various foundations [ages].

How it began, how the first Sun had its beginning 2513 years ago—thus it is known today, the 22 of May, 1558.

Aztec calendar.

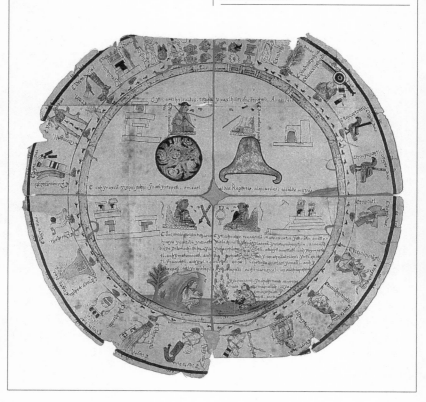

Codex depicting the cult of Tonatiuh, the sun god.

This Sun, 4-Tiger, lasted 676 years.

Those who lived in this first Sun were eaten by ocelots. It was the time of the Sun 4-Tiger.

And what they used to eat was our nourishment, and they lived 676 years.

And they were eaten in the year 13.

Thus they perished and all ended. At this time the Sun was destroyed.

It was in the year 1-Reed. They began to be devoured on a day [called] 4-Tiger. And so with this everything ended and all of them perished.

This Sun is known as 4-Wind.

Those who lived under this second Sun were carried away by the wind. It was under the Sun 4-Wind that they all disappeared.

They were carried away by the wind. They became monkeys.

Their homes, their trees—everything was taken away by the wind.

And this Sun itself was also swept away by the wind.

And what they used to eat was our nourishment.

[The date was] 12-Serpent. They lived [under this Sun] 364 years.

Thus they perished. In a single day they were carried off by the wind. They perished on a day 4-Wind.

The year [of this Sun] was 1-Flint.

This Sun, 4-Rain, was the third.

Those who lived under this third Sun, 4-Rain, also perished. It rained fire upon them. They became turkeys.

This Sun was consumed by fire. All their homes burned.

They lived under this Sun 312 years.

They perished when it rained fire for a whole day.

And what they used to eat was our nourishment.

[The date was] 7-Flint. The year was 1-Flint and the day 4-Rain.

They who perished were those who had become turkeys.

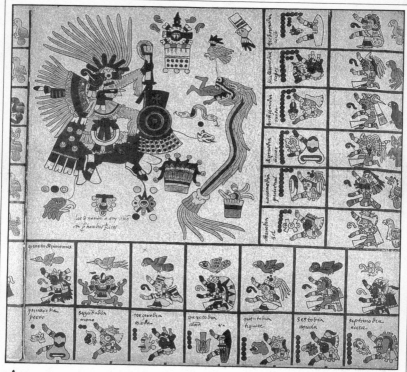

A month from the *Codex Borbonicus,* with the god Xipe Totec.

The offspring of turkeys are now called *pípil-pípil.*

This Sun is called 4-Water; for 52 years the water lasted.

And those who lived under this fourth Sun, they existed in the time of the Sun 4-Water.

It lasted 676 years.

Thus they perished: They were swallowed by the waters and they became fish.

The heavens collapsed upon them and in a single day they perished.

And what they used to eat was our nourishment.

[The date was] 4-Flower. The year was 1-House and the day 4-Water.

They perished, all the mountains perished.

The water lasted 52 years and with this ended their years.

This Sun, called 4-Movement, this is our Sun, the one in which we now live.

And here is its sign, how the Sun fell into the fire, into the divine hearth,

there at Teotihuacán.
It was also the Sun of our Lord
    Quetzalcoatl in Tula.
The fifth Sun, its sign 4-Movement,
is called the Sun of Movement because
    it moves and follows its path.
And as the elders continue to say, under
    this Sun there will be earthquakes
    and hunger, and then our end shall
    come.

> Quoted in Miguel León-Portilla
> *Aztec Thought and Culture*
> 1982

*The Aztec calendar stipulates that the
world collapsed four times. The present
world, the fifth, was said to have been
born on 4-*Ollin.

In the traditions and chronicles written
up after the conquest as well as in pre-
Columbian manuscripts and in the bas-
reliefs of some monuments, one
encounters the idea that our world was
preceded by four worlds or "suns"
which ended in cataclysms. These
vanished worlds are called the "Tiger
Sun" (*Ocelotonatiuh*), "Wind Sun"
(*Eecatonatiuh*), "Rain Sun"
(*Quiauhtonatiuh*), and "Water Sun"
(*Atonatiuh*). The Rain Sun is also
sometimes known as the "Fire Sun"
(*Tletonatiuh*), because it was a rain of
fire that destroyed the world at the end
of this period.

These four ages are not always
described in the same order of
succession. According to the *Anales de
Cuauhtitlán*, the first of the suns was
the Water Sun, followed by those of the
Tiger, Rain, and Wind. The *Historia de
los Mexicanos por sus Pinturas* gives the
following order: Tiger, Wind, Rain,
Water, which is corroborated by the
magnificent monument known as the

Relighting the fire in the temple.

"Aztec Calendar." This famous bas-
relief, like those of the "stone of the
suns," enumerates the four ages in the
same order as the *Historia*, each age
represented by a date, that of the cataclysm that ended it. These dates are:

4-*Ocelotl* (4-Tiger), end of the
Tiger Sun.

4-*Eecatl* (4-Wind), end of the Wind
Sun.

4-*Quiauitl* (4-Rain), end of the
Rain Sun.

4-*Atl* (4-Water), end of the Water
Sun.

Finally, our present world is marked
on the Aztec Calendar by the date of
4-*Ollin* (4-Movement, or Earthquake),
when our sun began moving, four days
after its birth. In the ritual calendar,
this is the festival of the sun and of the
lords. But it is also probably the date
when our world will end in earth-
quakes, the sign *ollin* symbolizing both
the sun's movement and seismic shocks.

In the *tonalamatl*, or divinatory
calendar, all days bearing the number 4
are considered an ill omen. The day of
4-*Ocelotl*, end of the Tiger Sun, is a day
of ill omen, dominated by the god
Tezcatlipoca. Tezcatlipoca, god of the
north, of cold, and of night, turned

himself into a tiger, according to the *Historia de los Mexicanos*, to throw down the sun. The first age, according to the *Anales de Cuauhtitlán*, ended in cold and darkness, following an eclipse.

The date 4-*Eecatl*, end of the Wind Sun, is considered a day of enchantments and sorcery. The day 1-*Eecatl* is the day of the sorcerer *par excellence*. In fact, it was by a vast magic operation that the second world ended: All men were turned into monkeys. At the same time a violent wind was blowing, the manifestation of *Eecatl*, god of the wind, who is one of the forms of Quetzalcoatl. The idea that the men of one of the vanished worlds were changed into monkeys is also found in the great Quiché Maya chronicle, the *Popol-Vuh*. Among Central Mexicans, this idea was linked to the actions of the god Quetzalcoatl in the form of the wind divinity, protector of magicians.

The date 4-*Quiauitl*, end of the Rain Sun, is placed under the protection of Tláloc, god of rain, and it is this god's mask, recognizable by its long teeth and enormous eyes, that is used as the sign of rain. The third world collapsed under a rain of fire. Tláloc was not only god of rain, although this was his most usual function, but also god of fire that falls from the sky—lightning and thunder, and perhaps volcanic eruptions; this is the rain of fire (*tlequiauitl*).

The date 4-*Atl*, end of the Water Sun, is represented on the monuments mentioned above by the number 4 accompanied by the face of the goddess Chalchiuhtlicue, "she who wears a skirt of precious stone," a water divinity and companion of Tláloc; she seems to emerge from a receptacle. Here, one is

The long migration of the ancient Mexicans to Tenochtitlán.

clearly dealing with water, because the fourth world ended in inundations, in a kind of flood.

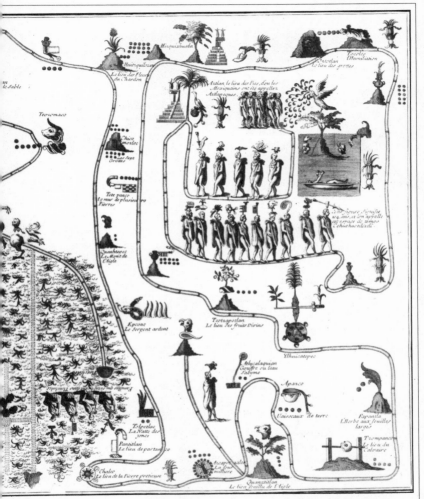

Thus, on four occasions, a world was born and collapsed in gigantic catastrophes. Today's world will suffer the same fate. The ancient Mexicans conceived this history of the universe as that of victories and defeats of the alternating principles, taking turns to rule over everything, then driven away and deprived of any grip on the real world. The first of the suns is that of Tezcatlipoca; this is the age of cold, the night, the north. The second, under the

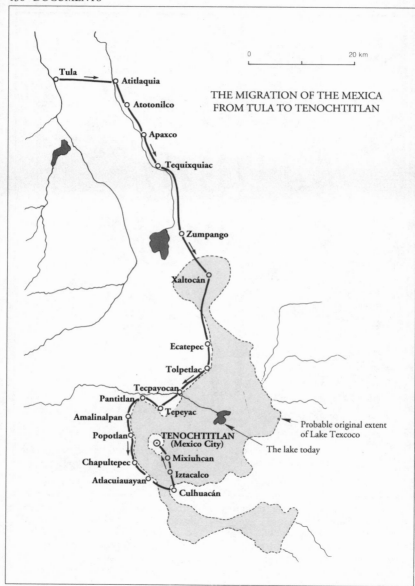

THE MIGRATION OF THE MEXICA
FROM TULA TO TENOCHTITLAN

0   20 km

Tula

Atitlaquia

Atotonilco

Apaxco

Tequixquiac

Zumpango

Xaltocán

Ecatepec

Tolpetlac

Tecpayocan

Pantitlan

Amalinalpan

Tepeyac

Popotlan

TENOCHTITLAN
(Mexico City)

Chapultepec

Mixiuhcan

Iztacalco

Atlacuiauayan

Culhuacán

Probable original extent
of Lake Texcoco

The lake today

influence of Quetzalcoatl, god of the west, is the period of sorcery and of the west. The third is dominated by Tláloc who, as god of rain, is a divinity of the south. The fourth, sun of water and of Chalchiuhtlicue, is a period of the east, because water and its goddess belong to the east. As for today's sun, the fifth, it is the sun of the center because five is the number of center; the divinity of the center is Xiuhtecutli, god of fire: Hence our sun is a fire-sun, sometimes represented by the same symbol as fire, a butterfly....

The tradition concerning the four suns is just one example of the way people think in every area: The interpretation of all the phenomena in the world through the alternation of fundamental aspects of reality which follow and replace each other, triumph and disappear, and which are linked to the directions of space.

The cosmogonic myths contain few indications as to the way they envisaged the world's inhabitants in these vanished epochs. There was generally a belief that there were giants in those days, then men who lived on wild grasses. The ancient Mexicans had a very clear sense of the superiority of their agricultural civilization over that of the nomadic tribes, the Chichimecs, who wandered in the semi-desert region of the north. They themselves, before reaching the central plateau, had led this precarious way of life.... As opposed to the civilization of maize, of which they were the trustees, they depicted their ancestors of the dead suns as barbarians who were ignorant of agriculture....

Between the end of the fourth sun and the start of ours, they placed a transitional period, supposed to have lasted twice-times-thirteen years: the years, in the count of time, are divided into series of thirteen, each of these series being attached to one of the cardinal points: in four 13s, a native "century," the 52-year cycle, was completed.

The "fall of the sky," no doubt the deluge that put an end to the Water Sun, took place in the year 1-*Tochtli* (1-Rabbit), the year of the south. The gods Quetzalcoatl and Tezcatlipoca undertook the raising of the sky; and when the task was completed, Tezcatlipoca changed his name, becoming Mixcoatl, god of the north, in the year 2-*Acatl* (2-Reed): In the divinatory calendar, the day 2-*Acatl* was devoted to Tezcatlipoca. During the eighth year the *macehualtin* were created, the working men. Men were needed for the future sun, men destined to be sacrificed and to nourish the heavenly body with their blood.

With the second thirteen years, which starts with the year 1-*Acatl*, one enters the domain of the east. *Ce acatl* (1-*Acatl*-Reed) is the cyclic name of Quetzalcoatl, as god of the east and of the morning star, of resurrection. All of the fifth sun will be dominated by this great theme of death and rebirth, of the sacrifice necessary to the life of the heavenly bodies and of the universe. In the year 1-*Acatl*, the gods decide to create the sun. But for that it is already necessary to spill blood, liberate the life forces; and one can only liberate them by killing, by sacrifice, and by war. The gods unleash war, taking part themselves on occasions. The last year of the second series, 13-*Acatl*, is that of the sun's birth.

Jacques Soustelle
The Universe of the Aztecs, 1979

The Creation of Man and Woman

After the sun had been created, the gods wondered who would inhabit the earth.

And then Quetzalcoatl went to *Mictlan*. He approached Mictlantecuhtli and Mictlancíhuatl [Lord and Lady of the region of the dead]....

"I come in search of the precious bones in your possession. I have come for them."

And Mictlantecuhtli asked of him, "What shall you do with them, Quetzalcoatl?"

And once again Quetzalcoatl said, "The gods are anxious that someone should inhabit the earth."

And Mictlantecuhtli replied, "Very well, sound my shell horn and go around my circular realm four times."

But his shell horn had no holes. Quetzalcoatl therefore called the worms, who made the holes. And then the bees went inside the horn and it sounded.

Upon hearing it sound, Mictlantecuhtli said anew, "Very well, take them."

But Mictlantecuhtli said to those in his service, "People of *Mictlan!* Gods, tell Quetzalcoatl that he must leave the bones."

Quetzalcoatl replied, "Indeed not; I shall take possession of them once and for all."

And he said to his *nahualli* [double], "Go and tell them that I shall leave them."

And the *nahualli* said in a loud voice, "I shall leave them."

But then he went and took the precious bones. Next to the bones of man were the bones of woman; Quetzalcoatl took them....

Tzapotla Tena, one of the Aztec gods.

And again Mictlantecuhtli said to those in his service, "Gods, is Quetzalcoatl really carrying away the precious bones? Go and make a pit."

The pit having been made, Quetzalcoatl fell in it; he stumbled and was frightened by the quail. He fell dead and the precious bones were scattered. The quail chewed and gnawed on them.

Then Quetzalcoatl came back to life; he was grieved and he asked of his *nahualli*, "What shall I do now...?"

And the *nahualli* answered, "Since things have turned out badly, let them turn out as they may."

And he gathered them…and then he took them to *Tamoanchan*.

And as soon as he arrived, the woman called Quilaztli, who is Cihuacóatl, took them to grind and put them in a precious vessel of clay.

Upon them Quetzalcoatl bled his member. The other gods and Quetzalcoatl himself did penance.

And they said, "People have been born, oh gods, the *macehuales* [those given life or 'deserved' into life through penance]."

Because, for our sake, the gods did penance!

1558 Mexican manuscript
Quoted in León-Portilla, *op. cit.*

The maguey, from which the Indians extracted juice to make pulque.

Duties and Responsibilities

Speeches, poems, and precepts reveal the Indians' conception of existence and the duties of everyone on earth.

Act! Cut wood, work the land,
   plant cactus, sow maguey;
You shall have drink, food, clothing.

With this you will stand straight.
With this you shall live.
For this you shall be spoken of, praised;
In this manner you will show yourself
   to your parents and relatives.
Someday you shall tie yourself to a skirt
   and blouse.
What will she drink? What will she eat?
Is she going to live off the air?
You are the support, the remedy;
You are the eagle, the tiger.

Receive this word, listen to this word.
I hope that for a little time you will live

with Our Lord,
He who is Master of the Close Vicinity.
Live on earth;
I hope you will last for a little time.
Do you know much?
With good judgment, look at things,
   observe them wisely.
It is said that this is a place of hardship,
   of filth, of troubles.
It is a place without pleasure, dreadful,
   which brings desolation.

There is nothing true here.…
Here is how you must work and act;
Safely kept, in a locked place,
   the elders left us these words
   at the time of their departure.
Those of the white hair and the
   wrinkled faces,
   our ancestors.…
They did not come here to be arrogant;

They were not seeking;
They were not greedy.
They were such
   that they were highly esteemed on
   earth;
They came to be eagles and tigers.

Do not throw yourself upon women
   like the dog which throws itself upon
   food.
Be not like the dog
   when he is given food or drink,
   giving yourself up to women before
   the time comes.

Even though you may long for women,
   hold back, hold back with your heart
   until you are a grown man, strong
   and robust.
Look at the maguey plant.
If it is opened before it has grown
   and its liquid is taken out,
   it has no substance.
It does not produce liquid; it is useless.
Before it is opened
   to withdraw its water,
   it should be allowed to grow and
   attain full size.
Then its sweet water is removed
   all in good time.

This is how you must act:
   before you know woman
   you must grow and be a complete
   man.
And then you will be ready for
   marriage;
   you will beget children of good
   stature, healthy, agile, and comely....
      Indian poems by Andrés de Olmos
      Quoted in León-Portilla, *op. cit.*

At dawn the judges would be seated on
their mats, and soon people would
begin to arrive with their quarrels.

Education of children and adolescents in a scene from the *Codex Mendoza*.

Somewhat early, food would be brought from the palace. After eating the judges would rest a while, and then they would continue to listen until two hours before the sun set. In matters of appeal there were twelve judges who had jurisdiction over all the others, and they used to sentence with the sanction of the ruler.

Every twelve days the ruler would meet with all of the judges to consider all of the difficult cases.... Everything that was taken before him was to have been already carefully examined and discussed. The people who testified would tell the truth because of an oath which they took, but also because of the fear of the judges, who were very skilled at arguing and had a great sagacity for examination and cross-examination. And they would punish those who did not tell the truth.

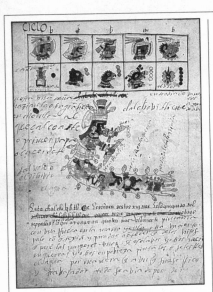

Tláloc, god of rain.

a false account to the lord of Texcoco, it was ordered that he be strangled and that the trial begin anew. And thus it was done, and the verdict was in favor of the common man.

Narrative by Alonso de Zurita,
Bernardino de Sahagún's informant,
Quoted in León-Portilla, *op. cit.*

The Myth of Quetzalcoatl

Quetzalcoatl was held in high esteem and considered to be god; he was worshiped at Tula from the remotest time. His very high temple had been a staircase with steps so narrow that a foot could not get a firm hold. His statue was always in a recumbent position and covered with *mantas* [tapestries]. His face was very ugly, bearded, with an elongated head. His servants or subjects were all workers in the mechanical arts, and very skilled at working the green stone called *chalchiuitl*, melting silver, and many other crafts of this kind.

All these trades had their source and origin in Quetzalcoatl, who possessed houses made of the precious stone called *chalchiuitl*, or constructed of silver, red and white mother-of-pearl, boards, turquoise, and rich featherwork. His subjects were very quick to reach any place wherever it was. There is a hill called Tzatzitepetl (it is still called this today) where there lived a public crier whose job it was to make announcements. He could be heard in the towns and villages even a hundred leagues away in the Anáhuac. They heard his voice over these long distances, and immediately hurried to see what Quetzalcoatl desired.

It is also said that this god was very rich, and that he had all manner of food and drink; his maize was very

The judges received no gifts in large or small quantities. They made no distinction between people, important or common, rich or poor, and in their judgments they exercised the utmost honesty with all. And the same was true of the other administrators of the law.

If it were found that one of them had accepted a gift or misbehaved because of drinking, or if it were felt that he was negligent…the other judges themselves would reprehend him harshly. And if he did not correct his ways, after the third time they would have his head shorn. And with great publicity and shame for him they would remove him from office. This was a great disgrace…. And because one judge showed favoritism in a dispute toward an important Indian against a common man and gave

Quetzalcoatl

abundant, his calabashes as big around as an armspan; his maize cobs were so long that their length was measured in armspans; the white-beet stalks too were very long, and so big you could climb them like a tree. All colors of cotton were sown and gathered—red, scarlet, yellow, brown, whitish, green, blue, black, dark, orange, and buff, with the peculiarity that these colors ...originated from the plant.

It is also said that in the above-mentioned town of Tula, many types of richly feathered birds were bred, in a great variety of colors, which are called *xiuhtototl, quetzaltototl, çaquan,* and *thauhquechol,* and many others besides which had the sweetest of songs.

Quetzalcoatl, moreover, possessed all the riches of the world, in gold and silver, in green stones called *chalchiuitl,* and in other precious things, as well as a great abundance of cacao trees of different colors. [His] vassals were very rich and wanted for nothing; there was no shortage of food, no lack of maize....

It is also said that Quetzalcoatl underwent penance by pricking his legs and withdrawing blood with which he coated thorns of maguey. He washed at midnight in a fountain called *xicapoyan,* and it was from this that the priests and ministers of the Mexican idols later adopted Quetzalcoatl's custom in the town of Tula.

Time put an end to the fortune of Quetzalcoatl and the Toltecs; because three sorcerers came against them, called Uitzilopochtli, Titlacauan, and Tlacauepan, who carried out a great number of tricks in the town of Tula.

It was Titlacauan who began, in the disguise of a white-haired old man. In this form he went to Quetzalcoatl's palace where he said to his pages: "I want to see the king and speak to him." "Get out!" was the reply. "Clear off, old man, you can't see him; he's ill; you would just annoy him and disturb him." So the old man said: "I must see him." The pages replied: "Wait."

So they went to tell Quetzalcoatl that an old man wanted to speak to him, and they added: "Lord, we showed him the door so he would go away, but he refuses to go, and says he absolutely must see you." Quetzalcoatl replied: "Let him enter and come to me; I've been waiting for him for several days."

The old man was called; he entered the place where Quetzalcoatl was, and said to him: "How are you, my son? I have brought a medicine for you to drink." Quetzalcoatl replied: "Welcome, old man, I've been waiting for you for several days." He asked Quetzalcoatl: "How are you, how is your health?" Quetzalcoatl replied: "I am very poorly; my whole body hurts; I can't move my feet or hands." So the old man said to the king:

A fanciful 19th-century engraving depicting offerings to Quetzalcoatl (also opposite) of animal blood (piglet and fledglings) and human blood (by bleeding the ear and tongue).

"My lord, look at this; the medicine I've brought you is good…whoever drinks it feels drunk; if you want to drink of it, it will intoxicate you while healing you, softening your heart and turning your thoughts to the distressing fatigues of death, or of your departure."

Quetzalcoatl replied: "O old man, where must I go?" The old man answered: "You absolutely must go to Tullan-Tlapallan, where another old man awaits you; you will talk together, and, on your return, you will be changed into a youth; you will even return to a second childhood."

On hearing these words, Quetzalcoatl's heart was filled with great emotion. The old man added: "Lord, drink this medicine." "I don't want to drink it," said Quetzalcoatl. But the old man insisted: "Drink, lord," he said, "because, if you don't, you'll want to do so later; raise it, at least, to your forehead and drink a drop of it."

Quetzalcoatl tasted it, and then drank it, crying: "What is it? It seems to be very good and tasty stuff; it's cured me; I'm not ill any more; my health has returned." "Another sip," said the old man, "Drink again, for it is good and you'll be better afterward." So Quetzalcoatl drank again and got drunk. He began to cry sadly, and his softened heart abandoned itself to the idea of departing, and the old sorcerer's trickery, which had duped him, never let him shake off this thought.

The medicine that Quetzalcoatl drank was none other than the local white wine, made with magueys, called *teometl*.

Bernardino de Sahagún, *Florentine Codex: General History of the Things of New Spain,* 16th century

Indigenous Society

Aztec civilization had a rigorous social organization. At the top there reigned the tlatoani, *"he who speaks," who was elected by his peers, and the* tecutli, *the "princes." At the bottom were the* macehualli, *the "commoners," those who obeyed. In the middle, or on one side, quite separate, there were the* pochteca, *who traded and spied on the emperor's behalf, and the artisans, who bore the name of the glorious ancestors:* tolteca.

The Toltec Model

In the 16th century, after the Spanish conquest, Bernardino de Sahagún gathered embellished accounts about mythical Tula from the Aztec elders.

Truly they were all there together,
lived there together.
The remains of what they made and left behind
are still there and can be seen, among them
the works not finished, among them
the serpent columns, the round columns of serpents
with their heads resting on the ground,
their tails and rattles in the air.
The mountain of the Toltecs can be seen there
and the Toltec pyramids, the structures of stone and earth, with stucco walls.

Temple of Tlahuizcalpantecuhtli, the morning star, at Tula.

Two-headed serpent in jade and mosaic.

The remains of Toltec pottery also are
  there;
cups and pots of the Toltecs can be dug
  from the ruins;
Toltec necklaces are often dug from the
  earth,
and marvelous bracelets, precious green
  stones, emeralds, turquoise….

The Toltecs were a skillful people;
All of their works were good, all were
  exact,
all well made and admirable.

Their houses were beautiful, with
  turquoise mosaics,
the walls finished with plaster,
clean and marvelous houses, which is
  to say,
Toltec houses, beautifully made,
beautiful in everything….

Painters, sculptors, carvers of precious
  stones,
feather artists, potters, spinners,
  weavers,
skillful in all they made, they
  discovered
the precious green stones, the
  turquoise;
they knew the turquoise and its mines,
  they found
its mines and they found the mountains
  hiding

silver and gold, copper and tin,
and the metal of the moon.
The Toltecs were truly wise;
They conversed with their own
  hearts.…
They played their drums and rattles;
They were singers, they composed songs
and sang them among the people;
they guarded the songs in their
  memories,
they deified them in their hearts.
  Quoted in León-Portilla, *op. cit.*

Warfare

*Tlacaélel, the brother of Moctezuma I,
sang the glory of Huitzilopochtli,
the divinity who gained ascendancy
over Quetzalcoatl and encouraged the
Aztecs in their warlike pursuits,
demanding from them in return a
tribute in blood.*

Huitzilopochtli, the young warrior,
who acts above! He follows his path!
"Not in vain did I dress myself in
  yellow plumes,
for I am he who has caused the sun to
  rise."

You, ominous lord of the clouds,
one is your foot!
The inhabitants of the cold region of
  wings,
Your hand opens.

Near the wall of the region of heat,
feathers were given, they are scattering.
The war cry was heard…Ea, ea!
My god is called the Defender of men.

Oh, now he moves on, he who is
  dressed in paper,
he who inhabits the region of heat; in
  the region of dust,
he whirls about in the dust.

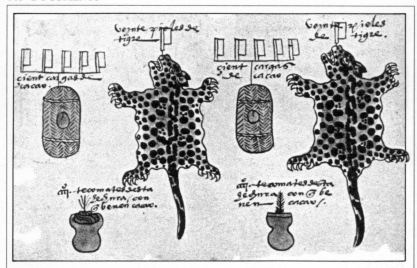

Items of tribute, including jaguar skins and containers of maize (above and opposite).

Those of Amantla are our enemies;
Come and join me!
With struggle is war made;
Come and join me!

Those of Pipiltlan are our enemies;
Come and join me!
With struggle is war made;
Come and join me!

Tlacáelel, speaking to Moctezuma I about the dedication of the Great Temple, remarked:

There shall be no lack of men to inaugurate the temple when it is finished. I have considered what later is to be done. And what is to be done later, it is best to do now. Our god need not depend on the occasion of an affront to go to war. Rather, let a convenient market be sought where our god may go with his army to buy victims and people to eat as if he were to go to a nearby place to buy tortillas …whenever he wishes or feels like it. And may our people go to this place with their armies to buy with their blood, their heads, and with their hearts and lives, those precious stones, jade, and brilliant and wide plumes… for the service of the admirable Huitzilopochtli.

This market, say I, Tlacáelel, let it be situated in Tlaxcala, Huejotzingo, Cholula, Atlixco, Tliluhquitépec, and Tecóac. For if we situate it farther away, in such places as Yopitzinco or Michoacán or in the region of the Huaxtecs, all of which are already under our domination, their remoteness would be more than our armies could endure. They are too far, and, besides, the flesh of those barbaric people is not to the liking of our god.

They are like old and stale tortillas, because, as I say, they speak strange languages and they are barbarians. For this reason it is more convenient that our fair and markets be in the six cities that I have mentioned.… Our god will feed himself with them as though he were eating warm tortillas, soft and tasty, straight out of the oven.… And this war should be of such a nature that we do not endeavor to destroy the others totally. War must always continue, so that each time and whenever we wish and our god wishes to eat and feast, we may go there as one who goes to market to buy something to eat…organized to obtain victims to offer our god Huitzilopochtli.

> Quoted in León-Portilla, *op. cit.*

Tribute

The subjects of the lords of Tenochtitlán paid all kinds of tribute—food, clothing, weapons.… The poorest among them, lacking what was necessary, offered their sons and daughters.

And as tribute they paid a great quantity of these feathers, feathers of all types and colors: green, blue, red, yellow, violet, white, and mixed colors. Innumerable quantities of cacao; enormous quantities of cotton bales, both white and yellow.

As for blankets, there were an amazing number. There were some of twenty armspans, some of ten, five, four and two, according to what each province could manage. Lords' blankets, very rich, made in different methods and styles, so rich and so magnificent that some had great edgings worked with color and feathers; others had great emblems; some had snake-heads, others lion-heads, and

Butterfly from the *Codex Florentino*.

others depictions of the sun. On others were skulls, blowpipes, idols; all were worked with threads of various colors and mingled with duck and goose feathers, those tiny velvety feathers, superb and strange.

Although they had no silk in this country, there were clothes made of worked and painted cotton, of great curiosity and beauty, made with great care and elegance. There were also blankets of agave thread, with which the Chichimecs paid tribute, worked and painted in colors with immense delicacy, decorated with emblems of golden eagles and a thousand other weapons and insignia; of these there were huge quantities.

These nations paid tribute to the Mexicans with live birds, the most precious kinds with rich plumage; some green, others red or blue; parrots, big and small, and all kinds of elegant colored birds, eagles, eagle-owls, sparrow-hawks, kestrels, crows, herons, geese, big goslings.

There were wild animals of all kinds: tribute was paid with live lions and tigers, and wild cats; all kinds of wild animals; they were brought in cages. Then snakes, big and small, poisonous and non-venomous, wild and tame.... It was really something to see, in cooking pots, all the kinds of serpents and creatures they paid tribute with! Even centipedes, scorpions, spiders, they asked for them in tribute, thus making themselves lords of every creature; everything was theirs, and belonged to them!

And what about the people on the coast? Every type of shell produced by the sea was brought in tribute: pectines, snails, big and little; curious fishbones, carapaces of freshwater and marine turtles, big and small; stones from the sea, pearls, amber, and granite; red and yellow, green, blue, violet, and pale green; all kinds of colors, scarlet, alum, some *nacazcolotl*, and some *zacatlax-calli*, which are plants with which they make colors, vitriol, dye-wood.

Other provinces paid tribute with hollow cups, big and small, some plain, others worked, and others gilded and painted in rich and curious designs that still survive: some are worked superbly. They also paid with big plain bowls which they have like we have silver plates, or big plates for carrying food to the table and for offering water to rinse the hands. They also gave handled cups, very surprising, like little cauldrons. In any case, they paid tribute with these cups and bowls of all kinds, big and medium, small and even smaller, made in different ways and styles of workmanship, and different shapes and colors.

Others paid tribute with women's

Some of the riches paid in tribute—feather crowns, clothing, and mats.

clothing, blouses and skirts, as superb and elegant as they could make them, full of wide edgings, astonishingly worked with various colors and designs, and feathers on the chest, wide emblems drawn with colored thread and, on the back, on others, they put worked roses; on yet others, imperial eagles; others were overlain with worked flowers so intermingled with feathers that they were a joy to see. Extremely rich skirts in price and value, superbly woven with excellent guile. Clothes that were worn by the wives and women of the lords and great men.

There was another type of women's clothing that was paid in tribute; all white, it was for the young and old women who served in the temples. Another type of garment for women, woven with agave thread, was distributed to servants. Mats of different kinds and designs were brought as tribute from other provinces; some of palms, others of furze; yet others made of broad and very shiny straw; other mats were made of canes, others of marsh-rushes. Tribute was also paid with seats, in the same way as with mats, with backs that were chiseled and worked with great elegance.

From other provinces tribute was paid with maize and beans, with *chia* (a type of sage)…and with pimentos of different species and kinds that exist and are cultivated in this land, and which are used for the different types and methods of stews they cook, by which they are differentiated and named. Great quantities of squash seeds were paid in tribute.

From other places, tribute was paid in cut wood, and tree bark which was used as fuel by the lords because of the fine embers it makes, and tribute was also paid with a great amount of charcoal which came from all peoples who lived near mountains.

Other people paid tribute in stone, lime, wood, planks, and beams for building their houses and temples. From other regions and provinces were brought deer, rabbits, and quails, some fresh, others roasted. Tribute was paid with moles, weasels, and big mice that we call rats, which are raised in the mountains.

Others paid tribute with grilled crayfish and ants, those big winged ants, and crickets, and all the tiny creatures that live on the earth. Thus, those living near lagoons paid tribute with all that grows in and around lagoons, even the silt and the flies that wander above, up to and including the water-mites and worms.

Then the peoples who had fruits… paid tribute with all the kinds of fruit there are in these provinces: pineapples, bananas, marmalade plums. In others, a thousand kinds of sapodillas, and treats produced in these provinces from guavas, yellow, black and white plums, avocados, and potatoes of two or three kinds.

These provinces paid tribute every day with great loads of roses, made and prepared with a thousand different kinds, because in Tierra Caliente there are very many types with a very strong perfume, some better than others, with a delicate perfume. They also brought the trees of these roses, with their roots, to plant them in the lords' houses, and all this was a tribute meant only to display the Mexicans' grandeur and authority, and show that the lords had power to name and keep all that is created in water as well as on land.

So much for clothing and food; but there were provinces that paid tribute in armor made of cotton, very well stuffed and padded so that neither arrows nor spears could pierce them; shields made of woven sticks, so solid and thick that a sword could not make a hole in them. The front of these shields was very elegantly decorated with feathers of all colors…. Very beautiful armor, and depictions of ancient feats by their ancient lords and idols, which they use and still keep today in memory of their antiques and past deeds and lords.

They paid tribute with big and thick bows; arrows of different kinds and types. They paid tribute with very well worked round stones for slings, and with innumerable slings; white and black blades for swords; flints for arrowheads and darts.

Finally, imagine everything imaginable that there could be in this land from which tribute was paid to Mexico. Including honeycombs and the very bees in their hives; big jars of white honey and the other brown kind; tree resin, torches for illumination; soot, for smearing oneself, and roucou. And those provinces lacking in provisions, clothing and all the above, paid tribute with young women, girls and boys, which the lords shared among themselves. The males were called slaves, the females were almost all taken as concubines and gave birth to the sons of slaves, to which some people refer. In their quarrels over claims, when they are at the end of their tether, they leave and put a stop to it by saying, "He's the son of a slave." And this means those born of these concubines who, in ancient times, were the tribute of certain peoples.

Diego Durán
The History of the Indies of New Spain
16th century

The Tlatelolco Market

Four days after his arrival in Tenochtitlán, Cortés took a tour of the city. Accompanied by his armed guards, he crossed the city and never wearied of admiring its wealth. Bernal Díaz del Castillo, Cortés' constant companion, gave this report.

On reaching the marketplace…we were astounded at the great number of people and the quantities of merchandise, and at the orderliness and good arrangements that prevailed, for we had never seen such a thing before. The chieftains who accompanied us pointed everything out. Every kind of merchandise was kept separate and had its fixed place marked for it.

Let us begin with the dealers in gold, silver, and precious stones, feathers, cloaks, and embroidered goods, and male and female slaves who are also sold there. They bring as many slaves to be sold in that market as the Portuguese bring Negroes from Guinea. Some are brought there attached to long poles by means of collars round their necks to prevent them from escaping, but others are left loose. Next there were those who sold coarser cloth, and cotton goods and fabrics made of twisted thread, and there were chocolate merchants with their chocolate. In this way you could see every kind of merchandise to be found anywhere in New Spain, laid out in the same way as goods are laid out in my own district of Medina del Campo, a center for fairs, where each line of stalls has its own particular sort. So it was in this great market. There were those who sold sisal cloth and ropes and the sandals they wear on their feet, which are

Aztec merchants on the way to town (top) and installed at Tlatelolco (above).

made from the same plant. All these were kept in one part of the market, in the place assigned to them, and in another part were skins of jaguars and lions, otters, jackals, and deer, badgers, mountain cats, and other wild animals, some tanned and some untanned, and other classes of merchandise.

There were sellers of kidney beans and sage and other vegetables and herbs in another place, and in yet another they were selling fowls, and birds with great dewlaps (turkeys), also rabbits, hares, deer, young ducks, little dogs, and other such creatures. Then there were the fruiterers; and the women who sold cooked food, flour, and honey

An 18th-century view of customers and merchants under the arcades of the market at Tlatelolco before the arrival of the Spanish.

cake, and tripe, had their part of the market. Then came pottery of all kinds, from big water jars to little jugs, displayed in its own place, also honey, honey-paste, and other sweets like nougat. Elsewhere they sold timber, too, boards, cradles, beams, blocks, and benches, all in a quarter of their own.

Then there were the sellers of pitch-pine for torches, and other things of that kind, and I must also mention, with all apologies, that they sold many canoe-loads of human excrement which they kept in the creeks near the market. This was for the manufacture of salt and the curing of skins, which they say cannot be done without it. I know that many gentlemen will laugh at this, but I assure them it is true. I may add that on all the roads they have shelters made of reeds or straw or grass so that they can retire when they wish to do so, and purge their bowels unseen by passers-by, and also in order that their excrement shall not be lost.

But why waste so many words on the goods in their great market? If I describe everything in detail I shall never be done. Paper, which in Mexico they call *amatl*, and some reeds that smell of liquidambar, and are full of tobacco, and yellow ointments and other such things, are sold in a separate part. Much cochineal is for sale too, under the arcades of that market, and there are many sellers of herbs and other such things.

They have a building there also in which three judges sit, and there are officials like constables who examine the merchandise. I am forgetting the sellers of salt and the makers of flint knives, and how they split them off the stone itself, and the fisherwomen and the men who sell small cakes made from a sort of weed which they get out of the great lake, which curdles and forms a kind of bread which tastes rather like cheese. They sell axes too, made of bronze and copper and tin, and gourds and brightly painted wooden jars.

We went on to the great temple, and as we approached its wide courts, before leaving the market-place itself, we saw many more merchants who, so I was told, brought gold to sell in grains, just as they extract it from the mines. This gold is placed in the thin quills of the large geese of that country, which are so white as to be transparent. They used to reckon their accounts with one another by the length and thickness of these little quills, how much so many cloaks or so many gourds of chocolate or so many slaves were worth, or anything else they were bartering. Now let us leave the market, having given it a final glance....

> Bernal Díaz del Castillo
> *The Conquest of New Spain*
> 16th century

The Arts in Aztec Society

Pre-Hispanic Aztec society had several categories of artist. Sahagún's informants collected songs of praise to the glory of a variety of skilled workers. Here are four examples.

The Feather Artist
Amantécatl: the feather artist.
He is whole; he has a face and a heart.
The good feather artist is skillful,
is master of himself; it is his duty
to humanize the desires of the people.
He works with feathers,
chooses them and arranges them,
paints them with different colors,
joins them together.

The bad feather artist is careless;
He ignores the look of things,
he is greedy, he scorns other people.
He is like a turkey with a shrouded
   heart,
sluggish, coarse, weak.
The things that he makes are not good.
He ruins everything that he touches.

Tarascan utensils, Michoacán.

Fresco by Diego Rivera (1942) depicting the arts of the Tarascan civilization of Michoacán—dyeing fabrics, painting frescoes, making a codex.

The Painter

The good painter is a Toltec, an artist;
He creates with red and black ink,
with black water....

The good painter is wise,
God is in his heart.
He puts divinity into things;
He converses with his own heart.
He knows the colors, he applies
    them and shades them;
He draws feet and faces,
He puts in the shadows, he achieves
    perfection.
He paints the colors of all the flowers,
as if he were a Toltec.

The Potter

He who gives life to clay:
his eye is keen, he molds
and kneads the clay.

The good potter:
he takes great pains with his work;
He teaches the clay to lie;

He converses with his heart;
He makes things live, he creates them;
He knows all, as though he were a
    Toltec;
He trains his hands to be skilful.
The bad potter:
careless and weak,
crippled in his art.

The Smith
Here it is told
how a work was cast
by the smiths of precious metals.
They designed, created, sketched it
with charcoal and wax, in order
to cast the precious metal,
the yellow or the white;
Thus they began their works.

If they began the figure of a living
    thing,
if they began the figure of an animal,
they searched only for the similarity;
They imitated life
so that the image they sought
would appear in the metal.

Perhaps a Huaxtec,
perhaps a neighbor
with a pendant hanging from his nose,
his nostrils pierced, a dart in his cheek,
his body tattooed with little obsidian
    knives;
Thus the charcoal was fashioned,
was carved and polished....

Whatever the artist makes
is an image of reality;
He seeks its true appearance.

If he makes a turtle,
the carbon is fashioned thus:
its shell as if it were moving,
its head thrust out, seeming to move,
its neck and feet

Hammering a piece of metal.

as if it were stretching them out.

If it is a bird
that is to be made of the precious
    metal,
then the charcoal is carved
to show the feathers and the wings,
the tail feathers and the feet.

If it is a fish,
then the charcoal is carved
to show the scales and fins,
the double fin of the tail.
Perhaps it is a locust
    or a small lizard;
The artist's hands devise it,
thus the charcoal is carved.

Or whatever is to be made,
perhaps a small animal, or a golden
    neckpiece
with beads as small as seeds
around its border,
a marvelous work of art,
painted and adorned with flowers.

Quoted in León-Portilla
Op. cit.

Human Sacrifices

Aztec pictograms, Aztec oral tradition, the chronicles of the Spanish conquerors— all agree that mass human sacrifice was an accepted and common practice among the Aztecs. How and why? Here are an account from the time of the conquest and two attempts at interpretation by modern authors.

The Spanish View: On the Horrible Human Sacrifices Practiced by the Aztecs

The people of Piru may well have had the edge over those of Mexico in killing children and sacrificing their sons—for I have neither read nor heard that the Mexicans had this custom—but in the number of men they sacrificed and in the horrible way they did it they surpassed the people of Piru and indeed all the nations of the world. And to show the state of blind misfortune in which the devil kept these people, I shall refer at length to the inhuman practice they had in these regions.

Firstly, the sacrificed men were obtained through war, and they did not perform these solemn sacrifices if there were no captives, and that is why, according to some authors, the sacrifices were called victims, because they were defeated; the sacrifice was also called *hostia, quasi ab hoste,* because it was an offering made by one's enemies, although the use of the two terms was extended to all manner of sacrifice. In fact, the Mexicans only sacrificed their captives to their idols; and their wars were usually waged to obtain captives for their sacrifices.

Hence, when they fought each other, they tried to keep their adversaries alive, to take them without killing them, in order to enjoy their sacrifice, and that was the reason given by Moctezuma to the Marquis del Valle when asked why, having such power and having conquered so many kingdoms, he had not subjugated the province of Tlaxcala, which was so close.

Moctezuma replied to this that there

were two reasons to explain why they had not pacified this province, which they could easily have done had they wished.

The first was to have something to exercise Mexican youth, to prevent it being raised in idleness and pleasure; the second and main reason was that he had reserved this province as a source of captives to sacrifice to their gods.

The method adopted for these sacrifices was that on this palisade of skulls.... They grouped those who were to be sacrificed, and at the foot of this palisade they carried out a ceremony with them, which involved putting them all in single file at the foot of it, with many guards surrounding them.

Then a priest would come out, dressed in an alb with a fringed hem, and he came down from the temple summit with an idol made of white-beet and maize mixed with honey, its eyes made of green pearls, and its teeth of maize seeds; he came down the temple steps as fast as he could, and climbed on to a great stone fixed on a very big cross in the middle of the court. This stone was called *quauhxicalli,* which means stone of the eagle.

The priest climbed up a little staircase in front of the cross and descended another on a different side, still with the idol in his arms; he then climbed up to where those to be sacrificed were located, and he went from one side to the other, showing this idol to each man, saying: "This one is your god."

When he had finished showing it to them, he descended the steps at the other side, and all those who were to die departed in procession to the place where they were to be sacrificed. There they found ready the ministers who were to sacrifice them.

The Great Temple of Tenochtitlán, at the top of which sacrificial rites (opposite) took place.

The usual method of sacrifice was to open the victim's chest, pull out his heart while he was still half alive, and then knock the man down, rolling him down the temple steps, which were awash with blood.

To understand this better, you must know that, at the place of sacrifice, six sacrificers came and were installed in this high rank; four to hold the victim's feet and hands, another for the throat, and one to cut the chest and extract the victim's heart. They were called *chachalmua,* which in our language is the same thing as minister of sacred things; this was a supreme rank, held in very high esteem among them, and inherited like a property.

The minister who had the function of killing, the sixth of the group, was considered and revered as a supreme priest or pontiff, whose name varied according to the period or the solemnities during which sacrifices were made; also, their vestments were different when they came out to exercise their office, varying with the moment.

The man of this rank was *papa* and *topilzin*; the costume and vestments were a red tunic of dalmatic style, with a fringed hem; a crown of rich green and yellow feathers on the head, and, in the ears, a kind of gold ring set with green stones; and under the lips, towards the middle of the chin, a piece of blue stone....

These six sacrificers came out, their face and hands coated in a very dark black; five had a very crimped and tangled hairstyle with bands of leather attached around the head, and on their forehead they wore small discs of paper painted in several colors; they were clothed in white dalmatics worked in black.

With this ornamentation they were dressed like the devil, and to see them come out with such an evil appearance frightened the people immensely.

The supreme priest carried in his hand a big flint knife, very pointed and wide; another priest carried a necklace of worked wood that looked like a snake. All six stood before the idol, prostrated themselves, and lined up near the pyramidal stone I described above as being just in front of the door of the idol's chamber. This stone was so pointed that when a sacrificial victim was thrown on his back against it, he was bent over in such a way that in dropping the knife to his chest it was very easy to open him up the middle.

Once these sacrificers were placed in order, they brought out all those who had been taken prisoner in the wars who were to be sacrificed at these festivals; accompanied closely by guards, they were made to climb those long staircases, all in rows, and totally naked, up to the place where one could see the ministers.

As they arrived in order, they were each taken by the six sacrificers, one by the foot, another by the other foot, one by the hand and another by the other, and were thrown on their back against this pointed stone, where the fifth minister threw the necklace round their throat, and the sovereign priest opened their chest with this knife, with a strange quickness, pulling out their heart with his hands and showing it, still steaming, to the sun, and offering it this heat and steam.

Then he turned to the idol, and

Human sacrifice.

threw it in its face; then they threw the victim's body down the temple steps; it rolled very easily because the stone was so close to the steps that there was not even two feet of space between the stone and the first step; hence, with a kick they threw the corpses down the steps.

In the same way they sacrificed all those available, one by one, and after they were dead and their corpses thrown down, they were picked up by their owners, the people who had actually captured them; they carried them off and shared them out and ate them, celebrating the ceremony with them; there were always more than forty or fifty of them, because they were men who were very skilled at taking prisoners.

All the other neighboring nations did the same thing, thus imitating the Mexicans in their rituals and their ceremonies in the service of their gods.

José de Acosta,
Natural and Moral History of the Indies, 1590

Two Modern Assessments of the Aztecs' Ritual Sacrifice

Jacques Soustelle, an expert on the Aztecs, postulates that human blood, the food of the sun-god, was the driving force behind their universe.

One has to say that the extent of bloody rituals in Mexico, far from stemming from an innate and continually increasing cruelty, on the contrary coincides with a social and cultural evolution marked by a softening of manners. This is certainly a paradox, but one which has to be faced because it is based on facts which are certainly known. Yet one must try to understand. To do this means escaping as far as one can from the gravitational field of our own civilization, and placing ourselves in the minds of the ancient Mexicans.

What dominates this universe, what penetrates its whole conception, is the idea that the machinery of the world, the sun's movement, the succession of the seasons, cannot be maintained and cannot last unless they are nourished with the vital energy held in "precious water," *chalchiuatl,* that is, human blood....

Four worlds, the four suns, have already perished before ours in cataclysms, and the one in which we live will also succumb. So men—more especially the people of the sun, the Aztec tribe—have to carry out a cosmic mission, to repulse day after day the assault of annihilation. And it is a miracle renewed at every dawn which makes the sun rise up once again —provided that the warriors and priests have offered its "nourishment," *tlaxcaltiliztli,* the blood and hearts of the sacrificed.

The idea therefore—pushed rigorously to its most extreme and (for us) monstrous consequences, but with a perfectly coherent logic—that led to this bloody civilization was not based on a more inhuman or more cruel psychological foundation than other cosmological ideas. What our minds find difficult to grasp is the link— apparently obvious and indisputable for the peoples of late Mexico— between the continuity of natural phenomena and the offering of blood. But we have to accept this notion as "given" in the same way as the shape of the house, ornament, or garment that characterize one culture and not another, or the choice of the phonemes used by one language and not its neighbor.

There is no necessity about it: It is only one of the very numerous ways in which humanity, faced with the mysteries of destiny, tries to comprehend them in order to extract from this vision a rule of action. All we can say is that, after a certain period, some peoples chose this weltanschauung among all those that were possible, whereas the peoples of the preceding phase, those of Teotihuacán and Palenque, had chosen another....

It would clearly be ridiculous to try and explain such "superstructures" (to use Marxist terminology) through economic and social "infrastructures."

Jacques Soustelle
The Four Suns, 1957

The metaphysical explanation of human sacrifice leaves many specialists perplexed. It is very possible that there could be other causes—material, economic, demographic—at the origin of this butchery.

Without seeking to find a single explanation of human sacrifice—an enterprise obviously doomed to failure —we can nevertheless place the emergence of systematic sacrificial practices in the central plateau in its wider context. As far as one can judge from historical and archaeological data, it seems to coincide with two contemporary events: on the one hand, the new arrivals reached the edges of Tula and found themselves in the presence of staked-out lands that had long been occupied by sedentary agriculturalists; deprived of pasture-lands, the former hunters were inescapably led to engage in a struggle against the indigenous owners.

On the other hand, at the entrance of the immense northern plains, the outskirts of the Valley of Mexico represent a narrow bottleneck; the territory shrinks, and demographic concentration increases. The ancient rivalries between Chichimec tribes, which previously found their solution in dispersal and reciprocal distancing, could not fail to be exacerbated in a context that necessarily tended towards promiscuity.

For all these populations of immigrants from the north, the struggle for living space had to be fought on two fronts: against the rival tribes, and against the original inhabitants. This continued until the *pax azteca* war was endemic throughout the [valley]. Human sacrifice, which is an appendage of war elevated into a system, quite naturally became its validation and ideological justification.

Christian Duverger
The Origin of the Aztecs, 1983

Temple of the Sun (below) at the top of which was the stone of sacrifices (right).

The Rough and Smooth of the Conquest

In 1519 Hernán Cortés reached the coast of Mexico, and less than two years later he had penetrated—and conquered— the Aztec empire.

The death of Moctezuma II, killed by his own people, according to Spanish legend.

Shortly before the Spaniards arrived, the whole Triple Alliance rumbled with stories announcing the imminent end of Moctezuma's reign.

He asked the king of Azcapotzalco for reinforcements and, when they arrived with their coils of rope and their tools, everyone began to pull, but the stone, without moving or giving the slightest sign of wanting to, again spoke: "Poor wretches, why do you work in vain? Haven't I told you that I won't reach Mexico? Go and tell Moctezuma that there is no more time; he has delayed too long in making up his mind. Tell him that he should have set about it earlier if he wanted to carry

The king of Texcoco, Nezahualpilli, announces the Spaniards' arrival to Moctezuma.

me off; I no longer need to go, because something else has been determined by divine wish. He should not oppose his destiny. Why should I go over there? To be subject afterward to ruin and contempt? Warn him that his power and his rule are ending, that he will soon see and experience for himself the end that awaits him for having wished to be greater than the god himself who determines things. So leave me because, if I start to move, it will be the worse for you."

Moctezuma did not wish to give any credence to the tale, which was related to him, although he was starting to feel some fear.

But soon there could no longer be any doubt. Everything agreed in predicting the arrival of the strangers and the end of Moctezuma. Could soothsayers and sorcerers confirm the disastrous omen?

The governors and village chiefs…sent numerous soothsayers, sorcerers, magicians, and enchanters who presented themselves to him and said, "Lord, we came at your beckoning to learn your wishes and see what you want of us." He replied, "Be welcome. You must know the reason why I've called you, I want to know if you've seen or heard or dreamed something concerning my kingdom and my person, since you are skilled at probing nocturnal space, traveling over mountains, piercing the enigmas of the waters, and scrutinizing the movements of the heavens and the course of the stars. I beg you to hide nothing from me, and to speak to me openly."

They answered: "Lord, who would be so impudent as to lie in your presence? We have neither seen nor heard nor dreamed anything concerning what you ask."

Moctezuma became angry, and said: "So your profession is to be swindlers, liars, to pretend that you're men of science and that you know the future, to trick everyone by claiming that you know everything that happens in the universe, that you have access to what is locked in the heart of mountains and at the center of the earth, that you see what is under the water, in caves and the fissures of the soil, in holes and in the gushing of fountains. You pretend to be children of the night, and all is lies and falsehood." And, in a terrible rage, he called his men at arms, and ordered them to throw them into cages and have them watched by a strong guard so they could not escape.

In prison these soothsayers and sorcerers did not show any despair but were full of joy and happiness, and they continually laughed among themselves. Moctezuma was informed of this and sent his officers to beg them to confess what they knew, promising them their freedom. They replied that, since he was so insistent on knowing his misfortune, they would tell him what they had learned from the stars in heaven and all the sciences in their power; that he was to be the victim of so astonishing a wonder that no man had ever known a similar fate. And, venting his anger and his ire, one of the oldest prisoners cried to everyone: "Let Moctezuma know that in a single sentence I want to tell him what will become of him. Those who are to avenge the affronts and sufferings he has inflicted and is inflicting on us are already on the march. And I will say nothing more, being content to await what must happen very soon."

Hence, when his informers warned him of the landing of Cortés' small troop, Moctezuma, convinced that he was dealing with gods, hurried to go and meet them.

Moctezuma, perched on a palanquin beneath a

When it was announced to him that Cortés' arrival was imminent, he had himself raised again on to the shoulders of the princes, as he had come, and went to meet him. Then, seeing the marquis, he slid from his hammock and stepped to the ground. Seeing this, Hernán Cortés dismounted from the horse on which he had come, and went to embrace him with great reverence. King Moctezuma did the same and taking each other by the hand, they went together to the sanctuary of the goddess Toci, which was beside the road, and where the powerful king and the marquis sat down on chairs prepared for them. Then the two other kings presented themselves, those of Texcoco and of Tacuba; one after the other they kissed the marquis' hands and offered him their necklaces and their roses, in accordance with their rank. And after them there came all the great men of the kingdom, making the same ceremonies and the same bows as to their god Huitzilopochtli.

Once this long and painstaking salutation was over, Moctezuma addressed the marquis, using Marina as interpreter, and bid him welcome in his city: He greatly rejoiced at his presence and at the sight of him, and recalled that he had replaced him on the throne and had governed the kingdom that his father, the god Quetzalcoatl, had left, holding—although unworthy to do so —the reins of power and receiving, in his name, the allegiance of his vassals; and if now the god was coming to reclaim his throne, he placed himself in his service and gladly abdicated, because the prophecies and tales of his ancestors had announced and promised this to him; let him recover his rights, if he so desired, Moctezuma would submit to his power; but if he had only come to visit him, he thanked him very sincerely and assured him that, to the bottom of his heart, he felt an intense pleasure and extreme joy because of this; he should rest and ask whatever he needed, his vassal would provide him with it in abundance.

Moctezuma affirmed his obedience, placing himself in his hands and in the service of His Majesty from that

...py, meets Cortés and his men.

welcomed him with humility and deference. And taking from the hands of one of the kingdom's nobles a very rich golden necklace, made of numerous plaques of gold and set with precious stones, he placed it round his neck and put in his hand a strange and superb plume of feathers worked into the shape of a rose. He also placed a garland of roses around his neck, and put on his head a crown of roses; then, moment on, and he expressed his desire to be instructed in the holy Catholic faith. And hence, after this long halt in this sanctuary or little temple, they left for the city of Mexico, the marquis on horseback and the powerful angry king carried in his palanquin as he had come, on the shoulders of his nobles.

Durán, *op. cit.*

The Taking of Tenochtitlán, as Told by Hernán Cortés to Charles V

This great city of Tenochtitlán is built on the salt lake, and no matter by what road you travel there are two leagues from the main body of the city to the mainland. There are four artificial causeways leading to it, and each is as wide as two cavalry lances. The city itself is as big as Seville or Córdoba. The main streets are very wide and very straight; some of these are on the land, but the rest and all the smaller ones are half on land, half canals where they paddle their canoes. All the streets have openings in places so that the water may pass from one canal to another. Over all these openings, and some of them are very wide, there are bridges....

Seeing that if the inhabitants of this city wished to betray us they were very well equipped for it by the design of the city, for once the bridges had been removed they could starve us to death without our being able to reach the mainland, as soon as I entered the city I made great haste to build four brigantines, and completed them in a very short time. They were such as could carry three hundred men to the land and transport the horses whenever we might need them....

There are, in all districts of this great city, many temples or houses for their idols. They are all very beautiful buildings.... Amongst these temples there is one, the principal one, whose great size and magnificence no human tongue could describe, for it is so large that within the precincts, which are surrounded by a very high wall, a town of some five hundred inhabitants could easily be built. All around inside this wall there are very elegant quarters with very large rooms and corridors where their priests live. There are as many as forty towers, all of which are so high that in the case of the largest there are fifty steps leading up to the main part of it; and the most important of these towers is higher than that of the cathedral of Seville....

There are three rooms within this great temple for the principal idols, which are of remarkable size and stature and decorated with many designs and sculptures, both in stone and in wood....

The most important of these idols, and the ones in whom they have most faith, I had taken from their places and thrown down the steps; and I had those

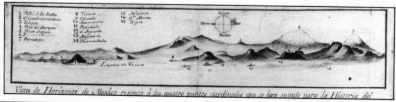

Vista de Horizonte de México respecto à los quatro puntos cardinales que se han sacado para la Historia del

THE ROUTES OF CORTÉS (1519–20)

- - - The march to Tenochtitlán in 1519
······· The retreat to Tlaxcala in 1520

GULF OF MEXICO

Cuautitlán • • Otumba • Ixtamixtlan • Zautla • Alto Lucero • Quiahuiztlan • Villa de la Veracruz
Tacuba • • Zotoluca • Cuyoaco
Texcoco • Tecoac • COFRE DE PEROTE • Jalapa • Cempoala
NOCHTITLAN • Hueyotlipan • 4282 • Alchichica • Coatepec
Ixtapalapa • Chalco • Tzompantepec • Ixhuacán • Jico • Rinconada
Xochimilco • Tlaxcala • Veracruz
Tlalmanalco • +IZTACCIHUATL +MALINCHE
Amecameca • 5286 Calpan • 4461
POPOCATEPETL + • Cholula • +ORIZABA • Xicalango
Cuernavaca • 5452 • Oaxtepec • Paso de Cortés • Tepeaca • 5747 • Cotaxtla

Izúcar de Matamoros

0   50   100 km

chapels where they were cleaned, for they were full of the blood of sacrifices; and I had images of Our Lady and of other saints put there, which caused Moctezuma and the other natives some sorrow. First they asked me not to do it, for when the communities learned of it they would rise against me, for they believed that those idols gave them all their worldly goods, and that if they were allowed to be ill treated, they would become angry and give them nothing and take the fruit from the earth, leaving the people to die of hunger. I made them understand through the interpreters how deceived they were in placing their trust in those idols which they had made with their hands from unclean things. They must know that there was only one God,

Lord of all things, who had created heaven and earth and all else and who made all of us; and He was without beginning or end, and they must adore and worship only Him, not any other creature or thing…and I urged them not to sacrifice living creatures to the idols, as they were accustomed, for, as well as being abhorrent to God, Your Sacred Majesty's laws forbade it and ordered that he who kills shall be killed. And from then on they ceased to do it, and in all the time I stayed in that city I did not see a living creature killed or sacrificed.

Seventy-five days of siege and skirmishes followed. Under the blows of Cortés, Aztec society disintegrated; Moctezuma was killed. His successor, Cuauhtémoc

The siege of Tenochtitlán. In this lakeshore city, built on a lagoon, whoever held the bridges would sooner or later be victorious.

(Guatimozin), soon had no more than a few faithful subjects around him. Here is the account of their surrender.

When it was light I had all the men made ready and the guns brought out. On the previous day I had ordered Pedro de Alvarado to wait for me in the market square and not to attack before I arrived. When all the men were mustered and all the brigantines were lying in wait behind those houses where the enemy was gathered, I gave orders that when a harquebus was fired they should enter the little of the city that was still left to win and drive the defenders into the water where the brigantines were waiting. I warned them, however, to look with care for Guatimozin, and to make every effort to take him alive, for once that had been done the war would cease. I myself climbed onto a rooftop, and before the fight began I spoke with certain chieftains of the city whom I knew, and asked them for what reason their lord would not appear before me;

for, although they were in the direst straits, they need not all perish; I asked them to call him, for he had no cause to be afraid. Two of those chieftains then appeared to go to speak with him. After a while they returned, bringing with them one of the most important persons in the city, whose name was Ciguacoazin, and he was captain and governor of them all and directed all matters concerning the war. I welcomed him openly, so that he should not be afraid; but at last he told me that his sovereign would prefer to die where he was rather than on any account appear before me, and that he personally was much grieved by this, but now I might do as I pleased. I now saw by this how determined he was, and so I told him to return to his people and to prepare them, for I intended to attack and slay them all; and so he departed after having spent five hours in such discussions.

The people of the city had to walk upon their dead while others swam or drowned in the waters of that wide lake where they had their canoes; indeed, so great was their suffering that it was beyond our understanding how they could endure it. Countless numbers of men, women, and children came out

Outside the city, on open water, the Spanish brigantines, equipped with artillery, devastated the flotilla of Mexican canoes.

toward us, and in their eagerness to escape many were pushed into the water where they drowned amid that multitude of corpses; and it seemed that more than fifty thousand had perished from the salt water they had drunk, their hunger, and the vile stench. So that we should not discover the plight in which they were, they dared neither throw these bodies into the water where the brigantines might find them nor throw them beyond their boundaries where the soldiers might see them; and so in those streets where they were we came across such piles of the dead that we were forced to walk upon them. I had posted Spaniards in every street, so that when the people began to come out they might prevent our allies from killing those wretched people, whose number was uncountable. I also told the captains of our allies that on no account should any of those people be slain; but they were so many that we could not prevent more than fifteen thousand being killed and sacrificed that day....

When I saw that it was growing late and that they were not going to surrender or attack I ordered the two guns to be fired at them, for although these did some harm it was less than our allies would have done had I granted them license to attack. But when I saw that this was of no avail I ordered the harquebus to be discharged, whereupon that corner which they still held was taken and its defenders driven into the water, those who remained surrendering without a fight.

Then the brigantines swept into that inner lake and broke through the fleet of canoes, but the warriors in them no longer dared fight. God willed that Garci Holguín, a captain of one of the brigantines, should pursue a canoe which appeared to be carrying persons of rank; and as there were two or three crossbowmen in the bows who were preparing to fire, the occupants of the canoe signaled to the brigantine not to shoot, because the lord of the city was with them. When they heard this our men leapt aboard and captured Guatimozin and the lord of Tacuba and the other chieftains with them. These they then brought to the roof close to the lake where I was standing, and as I had no desire to treat Guatimozin harshly, I asked him to be seated, whereupon he came up to me and, speaking in his language, said that he had done all he was bound to do to defend his own person and his people, so that now they were reduced to this sad state, and I might do with him as I pleased. Then he placed his hand upon a dagger of mine and asked me to kill him with it; but I reassured him saying that he need fear nothing. Thus, with this lord a prisoner, it pleased God that the war should cease, and the day it ended was Tuesday, the feast of Saint Hippolytus, the thirteenth of August, in the year 1521. Thus from the day we laid siege to the city, which was on the thirtieth of May of that same year, until it fell, there passed seventy-five days, during which time Your Majesty will have seen the dangers, hardships, and misfortunes which these, Your vassals, endured, and in which they ventured their lives. To this, their achievements will bear testimony.

Hernán Cortés
Letters from Mexico
1519–26

Cortés victorious at Tabasco, 18 March 1519, before arriving in Tenochtitlán.

The Aztecs, Defeated but Not Enslaved

In June 1524, almost three years after the fall of Mexico, a meeting took place between the Aztec leaders and Cortés, who was surrounded by Franciscan missionaries. Although the Aztecs made an act of allegiance, they nevertheless defended their spiritual values.

Our Lords, our very esteemed Lords:
great hardships have you endured to
    reach this land.

Here before you,
we ignorant people contemplate you....
Through an interpreter we reply,
we exhale the breath and the words
of the Lord of the Close Vicinity.
Because of Him we dare to do this.
For this reason we place ourselves in
    danger....

Perhaps we are to be taken to our ruin,
    to our destruction.
But where are we to go now?
We are ordinary people,
we are subject to death and destruction,

we are mortals;
Allow us then to die,
let us perish now,
since our gods are already dead....

You said that we know not
the Lord of the Close Vicinity,
to Whom the heavens and the earth
  belong.
You said that our gods are not true gods.
New words are these that you speak;
Because of them we are disturbed,
because of them we are troubled.
For our ancestors
before us, who lived upon the earth,
were unaccustomed to speak thus.
From them have we inherited
our pattern of life
which in truth did they hold;
In reverence they held,
they honored, our gods.
They taught us
all their rules of worship,
all their ways of honoring the gods.
Thus before them, do we prostrate
  ourselves;
In their names we bleed ourselves;
Our oaths we keep,
incense we burn,
and sacrifices we offer.

It was the doctrine of the elders
that there is life because of the gods;
With their sacrifice, they gave us life.
In what manner? When? Where?
When there was still darkness.

It was their doctrine
that they [the gods] provide our
  subsistence,
all that we eat and drink,
that which maintains life....

They themselves are rich,
happy are they,

things do they possess;
So forever and ever,
things sprout and grow green in their
  domain....
there "where somehow there is life," in
  the place of Tlalocan.
There hunger is never known,
no sickness is there,
poverty there is not.
Courage and the ability to rule
they gave to the people....

And in what manner? When? Where
  were the gods invoked?
Were they appealed to; were they
  accepted as such;
Were they held in reverence?

Above the world
they had founded
their kingdom.
They gave the order, the power,
glory, fame.

And now, are we to destroy
the ancient order of life?
Of the Chichimecs,
of the Toltecs,
of the Acolhuas,
of the Tecpanecs?

We know
on Whom life is dependent;
On Whom the perpetuation of the race
  depends;
By Whom begetting is determined;
By Whom growth is made possible;
How it is that one must invoke,
how it is that one must pray.

Hear, oh Lords,
do nothing
to our people
that will bring misfortune upon them,
that will cause them to perish....

Calm and amiable,
consider, oh Lords, whatever is best.
We cannot be tranquil,
and yet we certainly do not believe;
We do not accept your teachings as
  truth,
even though this may offend you.

Here are the Lords, those who rule,
those who sustain, whose duty is to
the entire world.
Is it not enough that we have already
  lost,
that our way of life has been taken away,
has been annihilated.

Were we to remain in this place,
we could be made prisoners.
Do with us as you please.

This is all that we answer,
that we reply,
to your breath,
to your words,
Oh, our Lords!

Quoted in León-Portilla
Op. cit.

Resistance to Christianity lasted for years,
as Andrés Mixcoatl's declaration before
the Tribunal of the Holy Office of the
Inquisition on 14 September 1537 shows.

My name is Andrés. I am a Christian. A
friar baptized me at Texcoco five years
ago. I don't know his name. I took
catechism every day at Texcoco with
the friars of St. Francis and their
disciples, some young men in their
charge. They told us in their sermons to
abandon our idols, our idolatry, our
rites; to believe in God; and many other
things. I confess that, instead of
practicing what they told me, for three
years I have preached and maintained

that the Brothers' sermons were good
for nothing, that I was a god, that the
Indians should sacrifice to me and
return to the idols and sacrifices of the
past. During the rainy season, I made
it rain. That is why they presented me
with paper, copal, and many other
things, including property.

I often preached in plain daylight at
Tulancingo, Huayacocotla, Tututepec,
Apan, and many other places. It was at
Tepehualco, about four years ago, that
I became a god. Since there was no rain,
during the night I made magic
incantations with copal and other
things. The next day it rained a lot.
That is why they took me for a god.
The *chuchumecas* executed one of their
priests, claiming that he knew nothing
and couldn't make it rain, I declare that
when I engaged in these superstitions
and magic practices, the devil spoke to
me and said: "Do this, do that." [In
another place] I did the same thing....

Why do you abandon the things of
the past and forget them, if the gods that
you worshiped then looked after you
and gave you what you needed? You
must realize that everything the Brothers
say is mere lies and falsehoods. They
have brought nothing to look after you,
they don't know us, nor we them. Did
our fathers and grandfathers know these
monks? Did they see what they preach,
this god they talk of? Not at all! On the
contrary, they are tricking us. We eat
what the gods give us, it is they who
feed us, shape us and give us strength.
Do we know these Brothers? I intend
to perform these sacrifices, and I'm not
going to abandon the habit because of
these people!

Quoted in Serge Gruzinski
Man-Gods in the Mexican Highlands
1989

Sorcery and Syncretism Under Spanish Domination

Victory by force of arms never ensures the domination of souls. In the 16th and 17th centuries, offerings and devotion to the old divinities coexisted strangely with worship of the Christians' one God.

Healers and Sorcerers

Domingo Hernández was from Tlaltizapan, a village on the right bank of the Yautepec River in Mexico. There he built up a reputation for holiness after he received from heaven the "virtue of healing illnesses." This was in the beginning of the 17th century.

When he was at death's door, two people dressed in white tunics appeared to him and took him very far from there to another place where there was a sick man, and there they blew on him. Then they led him to another place where they found another sick man,

Medicinal plants used by Aztec doctors.

Libro yndecimo.

palanj macaio, moteci oncan
contlalia in canjn palanj tunacaio, acopaltic, anoço teuhtic in vncan compachoa. 8.
¶ Naxi ivipil, anoço xoxoctic, ça tlanelhoatl, ololtontli, amo vei datlactic mjcoaio: auh mjcollo istac: injqujllo, iuhqujn istaquilid, quauhtla imuchioaia: icpati maqujque tlatlaci Auhinj muchioa chilla tulli, qujchioa, tamalli qujchioaa, yoā chilli, q. cenpoconja, conj incocoxquj, novaan. icpati imaqujn nixtleviac qujteci, çan cochpinja ichcatia mjxca.
¶ Tlalacaoatl, cantlanelhoatl, ololtontli, injcoaio tiltic, auhtic istac, injxiuhio xoxoctic, çan

and again they blew on him. They then told him:

"Let us return to your house for they already weep for you; rest now, for after tomorrow we will return for you."

At that moment, as he came to, he noticed that his friends were weeping for him as if he were already dead.

The two people dressed in white returned three days later. Like the first time, they took him to see the two sick men, and they blew on him just like before. Meanwhile, they told him:

"Hurry if you want to see your parents, your grandparents, and the rest of your family, but if they find you, you must absolutely not answer them; otherwise you will stay with them and you will not reach the world again."

Then he saw two roads, one very wide which many people took—that of the damned—the other narrow and steep, full of brush, rushes, and thorns. It was, they told him, the path of our Redeemer. He saw that few followed it, and again that many people took the broad path. The people in white tunics ordered him to follow them, and they arrived at the houses of the prodigies, where they told him:

"*Xitlamahuico*, look, and pay attention to what you see. Observe what happens to those who get drunk; beware, don't start your drinking again…(and many other things of that sort), otherwise you'll endure the same tortures. Give up pulque immediately or in three days you'll come back here. Now let's go to your house, for they are already weeping for you, and they should not be allowed to bury you."

They then told him:

"Listen, you who are poor and

Festival of pulque (fermented agave juice), a traditional Mexican alcoholic beverage.

miserable, here is what will give you food and drink in the world."

They taught him the words...which he has used ever since to care for people, and which brought him success in his treatments, even the most hazardous ones. Whereupon they took him back to his house. There he came to, and noticed people weeping for him as if he were dead.

He then said that, this same night, three ladies magnificently dressed in white, and only in that color, came to visit him, and he reported some of the words they had exchanged. According to him, it was the Virgin (Our Lady), Veronica and another lady whom he did not identify. Our Lady said that Christ Our Lord had captured this sick man, and she wanted to help him. Veronica obeyed her, and wafted some air to him with a piece of fabric. With that action he came to, and from that morning on he felt fine.

Hernando Ruiz de Alarcón
Treatise on Superstitions, 1629

The Spaniard and the Sorcerer

Puebla, 1665: Testimony of a Spaniard from Huamantla in the trial of the "idolatrous" Indians.

Six years ago, an Indian named Juan Coatl ("Cloud Serpent"), of the village of San Juan Ixtenco...told me he wanted to make me rich, as he had done for others. To that end I was supposed to go with him to the Sierra of Tlaxcala, where he would give me a good deal of gold and silver—provided I kept a "fast" consisting of staying away from women for two days before the Ascension. And in the event, driven by greed and curiosity to see whether the Indian would perform bad or superstitious acts, in the company of another Spaniard I climbed that mountain with Juan Coatl. When we got to a cabin that looked like a hermitage, the Indian lit candles and burned copal and incense in the hut. Then, leaving me there, he told me to wait and disappeared into the mountain reaches. He returned after some time and reproached me for not having come in good faith, because I had broken the promised fast and because I had a brother in the Church. That is why he would not give me the money I had sent him to find; that is why the master of those parts (a divine being of some kind) was incensed. In

B aptisms, funerals, and other Christian ceremonies were integrated with traditional Indian practices after the Spanish conquest.

spite of that, he would still get me quantities of things.

Seeing that the whole thing was a confidence game, I left the Indian. Four months later, I met him and asked why he had not kept his promise to make me rich, as he'd said he had done for others. He answered that the mountain was very angry because one of my brothers was a priest, and to calm its wrath he had gone up another mountain called the Caldera. There his protector had appeared to him as he slept, telling him to get up and go tell the people of Huamantla and San Juan (Ixtenco) that he had calmed down and was no longer angry with them for

having revealed his story: A heavy downpour that same day would be a sign. And if the Indian is to be believed, there really was a downpour.... I have heard the Indians say he is believed to be a high priest, that he marries and baptizes, choosing the name according to the day of birth on a calendar he has. He climbs to the Sierra of Tlaxcala with Indian men and women.

The truth according to the inquiry held by the ecclesiastical tribunal of the bishopric of Puebla.

Either by himself or with the intervention of some of the old *fiscales* of San Juan (Ixtenco), he gathers candles, copal, incense, and hens…and he goes up to the Sierra, or mountain of Tlaxcala, where they say he has a cave beside the spring that flows to San Juan Ixtenco, by way of Canoas: Two crosses mark the spot. At the entrance of the cave he lights candles, and inside he keeps idols, including a painted canvas representing an Indian woman with Indian youths at her feet, adoring her; another canvas delineating a figure with indigenous features, wearing a *tilma* (cape), with a stick in his hand; and two other paintings, one representing four snakes, and the other a large coiled serpent…. These are to be seen, along with other idols and a pile of garments offered in Juan Coatl's sanctuary….

Then he enters the cave with two other people, with lit candles and a great deal of copal. There they spend a day and a night in adoration of the idols…for Juan Coatl tells them these are their real gods, who give them water and good crops and all the other goods they possess, that they should believe in them and in an idol that he shows them, saying that she is their Virgin. They must not believe in the God of the Spaniards or in the Blessed Virgin. The times they must go "to the cave" he commands them to fast, which means abstaining from sleeping with their wives; and if by chance one of them disobeys, he treats them like "dogs who do not fast." One of them, among others, relates what happened to him for not having abstained on that occasion: When he returned to the village with him, Juan told him that he was nothing but a "dirty dog of a drunkard" who did not come fasting. The others were amazed at what he knew about what everyone was doing.

According to Coatl's wife, when he was about to go up the mountain he abstained the night before.

The Indians confessed, too, that when the parish priest came to the village, Juan reprimanded the children and adults who went to see him:

Doctor and patient (above). Opposite: One of the many representations of the Virgin of Guadalupe (see also overleaf).

Why go to the priest, since he was more than the priest, he spoke with the gods and provided for them what they needed? And he repeated that they should not believe in God but in their idols.

Quoted in Gruzinski
Op. cit.

The Healer and the Virgin

Yautepec, 11 September 1761: Interrogation of Antonio Pérez, the forty-year-old shepherd of the hamlet of Tlacoxcalco in the pueblo of Ecatzingo.

Four years ago, when I was living on the Gomez rancho at Tetizicayac in the jurisdiction of Atlatlahucan, I accompanied a Dominican father from there to the village of Yecapixtla. I do not know the name of the Dominican, where he comes from, or where he is. It could well be that he was the devil. I just remember that on the road the Dominican told me I was already damned because I drank far too much. Then he instructed me in caring for the sick, advising me to use…eggs, soap, milk, cooking oil, mint, or tomato skins, depending on the nature of the illness. He taught me cures for everything, including terrible toothaches, one of which consisted of making vapors by selecting six *tesontles* (volcanic rocks) of the same size and sprinkling them with water in which rue and artemisia had been cooked. Then they had to be taken and placed separately between the patient's legs.

For all my treatments I recite the Credo as the holy church teaches it, and I add these words: "In the name of the most holy Trinity, of the Father, the Son and the Holy Ghost. Amen." I put my trust first in God and only then in the herbs. When he is on his way to recovery, the sick man recites the act of contrition. I do all that because the Dominican friar told me to. That is how I cured Magdalena from Tetelcingo of typhoid fever, my wife Ana María of stomach pain, a certain Domingo, whose name and *pueblo* I do not know, of a leg wound.…

For six *reales* I bought from a painter named Bentura a very old painting, half an ell in size, which represented Christ. I kept it at my house and had it carefully cleaned. Many people came to offer him flowers and tapers. That is why Don Jacinto Varela, the priest of

Atlatlahucan, had me arrested. Afterward he freed me so that I would take him to my place and give him the holy Christ. As I was getting ready to do so, all of a sudden I found myself with my painting in a cave at the bottom of a ravine that runs along one side of Atlatlahucan. I had been carried there through the air, without knowing by whom, and I stayed in the cave for a moment before going to Chimalhuacan, where I gave the painting in question to the priest, who had it put under glass in his church. But since I accepted offerings of candles and money, the priest reprimanded me and put me out of the church.

Eight days later, in a place named Zabaleta, I met a *dieguino* [a barefoot Franciscan], who asked me to go with him to Puebla. I agreed, and all of a sudden found myself in the middle of the volcano, at the friar's side. The *dieguino* told me not to be sad about the holy Christ they had taken from me, because he would give me another, and in fact he gave me a head which seemed to be of glass, ordering me to make a body of cypress for it. I succeeded, with the help of a painter whose name I do not know, and I gave it the name of Santo Entierro [Christ of the Entombment]. I lit tapers before that Christ, recited some Credos and "Glory be." At the time of my arrest, I had that image at my house, and I do not know where it is now.

The same friar told me that in the volcano I would find a rainbow, and under the rainbow the Virgin; and that thereafter two new sources of water would appear at Chimalhuacan.

At the time, I disregarded his prediction and remained silent for a year and a half.

That time had passed when, sensing that I was giving up the ghost, I went to find Miguel Apparicio, Faustino, Antonio de la Cruz, and Pasqual de Santa María, to take them as witnesses to the cave. Once we got there, we saw a woman clad in a shining mantle and a body wrapped like a corpse. We did not touch it, and it is still in that condition. We knelt and recited ten Credos before making an image of *ayacahuite*, to which we gave the epithets of the Light, of the Palm, of the Olive, and of the Lily. That is what the *dieguino* friar had specified when I had spoken with him. He had also ordered that we make the image along the lines of the one in the cave—that is, the body that appeared to be dead. We were supposed to take it to the church of Yautepec and then to the cave, where we would find all the instruments of the Passion. Thirty-seven men were to accompany me in the undertaking.

Although the image was not brought to the church, I did take it to the cave in the company of five people from Ecatzingo: my son Matheo, his brother Felipe, María, Theresa, Diego, and twenty-five others from Izamatitlan, among whom were the *fiscal* Pedro, Pasqual de Santa María, and others whose names escape me.

When we got there, I discovered all the instruments of the Passion in a hole; they were made of terra-cotta, and I took them home. Pasqual de Santa María took the Virgin to his place, and we recited the rosary before her, and the "Glory be"; we danced and played music. That is what we were doing when the priest came in to arrest us.

Quoted in Gruzinski
Op. cit.

Mexican 16th-century church in typical baroque style.

The Descendants of the Man-Gods

Today their survival may depend on hostile city life.

"Before, few people went to Mexico City because they didn't know it," says Justino Esquivel. "Now the people from Mexico City think we go to sell things there because we don't want to work; and they even throw petrol on our fruits; but we go out of necessity. As long as the government gives us no work, we'll be forced to go there....

"In the city they move us on, they punish us, and then they throw us in prison; but tough, if we're doing it out of necessity, we're going to continue doing it. Under Uruchurtu [a mayor of the city known for his strict measures], as soon as they saw you in the street or sitting in a square, they took you: 'Come on, to jail with you! What are you doing there?' We have no papers. But when are they going to give us papers? They just have to see us [showing his old, worn-out clothes]. Yes, we're not going to lie, look at us. Are you going to say we're rich? It's just that, here, there's no way out, that's why we go to Mexico City."

Poor district of Mexico at the turn of the century.

On top of the difficulty of economic survival in the village, people stress the arduous nature of work in the fields, and the insecurity attached to it. One young man sums it up as follows:

"Here, there's no work, we earn nothing. We work with the boss from nine to nine, we sweat a lot to earn ten pesos. And the *zacatón* root [a type of Mexican fodder crop] is incredibly hard work. We start at six in the morning and get home at six in the evening, sometimes even at eight, completely covered in dust. It's a really filthy job…. That's why we go to Mexico City and, God willing, we'll continue to go there, because here we earn nothing."

The peasants of mixed origin, on the other hand, express other concerns.

"In twenty years time, nobody will be working the fields. I want a bit more for my children. They don't want to farm the land anymore, that's why we're leaving [for Mexico City]. They need to study because employers now ask for the certificate of secondary studies for a regular job…and here I can't give them all schooling [he has nine children], that's why I think I'm going to go to Mexico City."

In general, the Mazahua peasants, especially those who haven't lived there, have a very favorable opinion of the city, the notorious myth that attracts migrants to urban centers.

"I would be happy to leave for Mexico City or somewhere else, because you can earn good money there…."

But success in the city remains something mysterious, something that cannot be understood.

"I don't know if it's luck, I don't know why, but there are people who go to Mexico City, and immediately they go up in the world. And things go well for them. And there are others who stay a while and have to come back, they get nothing. Like me. I don't know if it's luck…." muttered one Indian.

Among migrants to the city, those who have succeeded in getting a decent income, and who have settled there, are happy they emigrated. In contrast, those who haven't found a permanent job and who live in great poverty in the seedy parts of town or the shanty towns complain bitterly about their situation.

Others, for their mental salvation, like those villagers who in their dreams make the city more beautiful, begin to imagine that village life is "more beautiful."

"If there was work at Dotejiare, I'd go back there. For most of the people there, things are all right, because they know how to run their affairs, they have good harvests…. The room where I live is lousy, it's better in Dotejiare. You're untroubled there, you have your house, even if it's small, you still have it…."

What emerges from this survey of different viewpoints is that the general tendency is not very subjective, except for the collection of myths exalting life in the city and in the countryside. For the most part they constitute fairly objective appreciations of the very concrete conditions that surround individuals. Hence, for example, the poorest Mazahua peasants do not even formulate a value judgment of migration; they limit themselves to putting it into practice.

Lourdes Arizpe
Migration, Ethnography, and Economic Change, 1978

Chronology

856	Founding of Tula by the Toltecs
1168	Destruction of Tula by the Chichimecs
	End of Toltec power
	The Mexica begin their journey
c. 1200	The Mexica arrive in the Valley of Mexico
1325	Tenochtitlán and Tlatelolco founded by the Mexica
1428	Formation of the Triple Alliance among Tenochtitlán, Texcoco, and Tacuba
1440–69	Reign of Moctezuma I
	First aqueduct to Tenochtitlán built
1445	Conquest of Oaxaca
1458	Conquest of Coixtlahuaca and Veracruz
1465	Conquest of Chalco
1469–81	Reign of Axayácatl
1476	Conquest of the Valley of Toluca
1481–6	Reign of Tízoc
1486–1503	Reign of Ahuítzotl
	Second aqueduct to Tenochtitlán built
1487	Consecration of the Great Temple at Tenochtitlán
1503–20	Reign of Moctezuma II
1503	Flooding of Tenochtitlán
1519	Cortés lands near Veracruz, arrives in Tenochtitlán, and is received by Moctezuma II
1520	Moctezuma II dies, a prisoner of Cortés
	The *Noche Triste*
1521	Fall of Tenochtitlán to Spain

Rulers of the Aztec Empire

Tenochtitlán		Texcoco	
1372–91	Acamapichtli		
1391–1414	Huitzilhuitl II	1409–18	Ixtlilxóchitl
1414–28	Chimalpopoca		
1428–40	Itzcóatl	1418–72	Nezahualcóyotl
1440–69	Moctezuma I		
1469–81	Axayácatl		
1481–6	Tízoc	1472–1516	Nezahualpilli
1486–1503	Ahuítzotl		
1503–20	Moctezuma II		
1520 (4 months)	Cuitláhuac	1516–9	Cacama
1520–2	Cuauhtémoc		

Further Reading

Acosta, José de, *Natural and Moral History of the Indies* (original 1590), Burt Franklin, New York, 1970

Aveni, Anthony, *Empires of Time: Calendars, Clocks, and Cultures,* Basic Books, Inc., New York, 1989

Berdan, Frances F., *The Aztecs,* Chelsea House, New York, 1989

Bray, Warwick, *Everyday Life of the Aztecs,* Hippocrene Books, New York, 1987

Coe, Michael D., *Mexico,* Thames and Hudson, London, 1986

Conrad, Geoffrey W., and Arthur A. Demarest, *Religion and Empire: The Dynamics of Aztec and Inca Expansionism,* Cambridge University Press, Cambridge, 1984

Cortés, Hernán, *Letters from Mexico* (original 1519–26), trans. and ed. by Anthony Pagden, Yale University Press, New Haven, Connecticut, 1986

Davies, Nigel, *The Aztecs: A History,* University of Oklahoma Press, Norman, 1980

————, *The Aztec Empire: The Toltec Resurgence,* University of Oklahoma Press, Norman, 1987

Díaz del Castillo, Bernal, *The Conquest of New Spain,* Penguin Books, New York, 1963

Diehl, Richard A., *Tula: The Toltec Capital of Ancient Mexico,* Thames and Hudson, London, 1983

Durán, Diego, *The Aztecs: History of the Indies of New Spain* (original 1581), Orion Press, Fort Lauderdale, Florida, c. 1964

Duverger, Christian, *L'Origine des Aztèques,* Seuil, Paris, 1983

Fagan, Brian M., *Kingdoms of Gold, Kingdoms of Jade: The Americas Before Columbus,* Thames and Hudson, London, 1991

Gibson, Charles, *The Aztecs Under Spanish Rule: A History of the Indians of the Valley of Mexico, 1519–1810,* Stanford University Press, California, 1964

Gruzinski, Serge, *Man-Gods in the Mexican Highlands: Indian Power and Colonial Society 1520–1800,* Stanford University Press, California, 1989

Hassig, Ross, *Aztec Warfare: Imperial Expansion and Political Control,* University of Oklahoma Press, Norman, 1988

————, *Trade, Tribute and Transportation: The Sixteenth-Century Political Economy of the Valley of Mexico,* University of Oklahoma Press, Norman, 1985

León-Portilla, Miguel, *Aztec Thought and Culture: A Study of the Ancient Nahuatl Mind,* trans. Jack Emory Davis, University of Oklahoma Press, Norman, 1982

————, *Broken Spears: The Aztec Account of the Conquest of Mexico,* Beacon Press, Boston, 1962

Lewis, Oscar, *The Children of Sanchez,* Random House, New York, 1979

Miller, Mary Ellen, *The Art of Mesoamerica: From Olmec to Aztec,* Thames and Hudson, London, 1986

Moctezuma, Eduardo Matos, *The Great Temple of the Aztecs: Treasures of Tenochtitlán,* Thames and Hudson, London, 1988

Pasztory, Esther, *The Iconography of the Teotihuacán Tláloc,* Dumbarton Oaks, Washington, D.C., 1974

Paz, Octavio, *The Labyrinth of Solitude,* Grove/Weidenfeld, New York, 1985

Sahagún, Bernardino de, *Florentine Codex: General History of the Things of New Spain* (original 16th century), 13 vols., University of Utah Press, Salt Lake City, 1970–82

Soustelle, Jacques, *The Four Suns,* Grossman Publishers, New York, 1971

————, *L'Univers des Aztèques,* Hermann, Paris, 1979

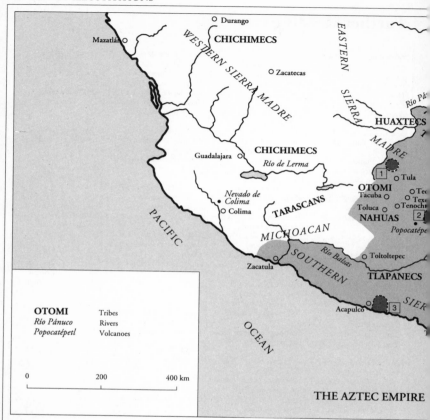

THE AZTEC EMPIRE

OTOMI — Tribes
Río Pánuco — Rivers
Popocatépetl — Volcanoes

0   200   400 km

List of Illustrations

Key: a=above; *b*=below;
l=left; *r*=right

Abbreviations: BAD=
Bibliothèque des Arts
Décoratifs, Paris;
BAN=Bibliothèque de
l'Assemblée Nationale,
Paris; BN=Bibliothèque
Nationale, Paris

Front cover Diego
Rivera. *Offering of Fruits,*
Tobacco, Cacao, and
Vanilla to the Emperor
(detail). Fresco, 1942.
Palacio Nacional,
Mexico
Spine Ceremony called
xocotl. Codex Borbonicus.
BAN
Back cover Aztec figurine
1 Cortés being placed in
command of the army.
Painting on copper after

Antonio de Solis. Museo
de America, Madrid
2 Three Spanish soldiers
during the first skirmishes
against the Indians of
Tabasco. *Ibid.*
3 Soldiers bringing
ashore anchors, cables,
and sails before obeying
Cortés' order for his own
fleet to be destroyed. *Ibid.*
4 Cortés' first meeting

with Moctezuma II's
envoys. *Ibid.*
5 Cortés entering
Tlaxcala. *Ibid.*
6 Cortés meeting
Moctezuma II. *Ibid.*
7 Moctezuma II pays
tribute to Cortés. *Ibid.*
8 The battle of Tepeaca.
Ibid.
9 Cortés takes Moctezuma
II prisoner. *Ibid.*

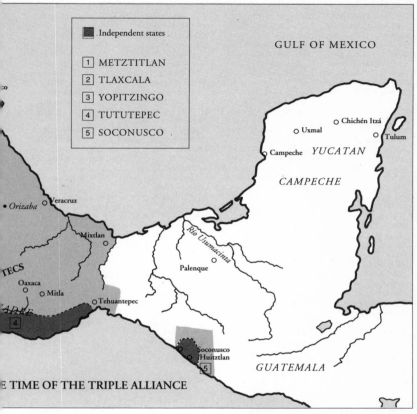

Independent states

1 METZTITLAN
2 TLAXCALA
3 YOPITZINGO
4 TUTUTEPEC
5 SOCONUSCO

GULF OF MEXICO

Chichén Itzá
Uxmal
Tulum
Campeche YUCATAN

CAMPECHE

Veracruz
Orizaba
Mixtlan

Río Usumacinta

Palenque

TECS
Oaxaca
Mitla
Tehuantepec

Soconusco
Huitztlan
GUATEMALA

E TIME OF THE TRIPLE ALLIANCE

Index